The Art Of Saying No

Take Back Your Power Without Guilt or Shame

Natalie Mills

1957 Publishing

The Art Of Saying No: Take Back Your Power Without Guilt or Shame

Cover Design by: Natalie Mills

Paperback ISBN:

Hardcover ISBN:

About the author

Natalie believes saying no isn't about pushing people away; it's about finally letting yourself come back home.

For years, she was the reliable one – the helper, the organiser, the "just one more thing" woman. If there was a gap to fill, a problem to solve, or a burden to carry, she stepped in without hesitation… and slowly stepped out of her own life in the process.

Her own turning point didn't arrive with fireworks or dramatic declarations. It came quietly – in moments of exhaustion, in the weight of too many yeses, and in the realisation that being everything to everyone had left very little room to simply be herself.

Instead of continuing to stretch herself thinner, Natalie began to explore something unfamiliar: boundaries. Not the rigid, cold kind, but the gentle, steady kind that protects your energy without closing your heart.

Dedication

This one is for me.

For the twelve-year-old girl
who folded her grief into responsibility
and wore strength like it was the only outfit she owned.

For the years spent saying yes
when my soul whispered no,
for the quiet erasing,
the gentle disappearing act
no one else seemed to notice.

I am still kind.
I am still loving.
But I am no longer leaving myself behind to prove it.

This is where I begin again –
with grace in one hand
and love in the other.

The Boundary Manifesto

I've said "yes" so often my tongue knows the way,
While my quiet "no" just kept fading away.
I've juggled their needs like a well-trained routine,
While losing the woman I used to have been.

My calendar's full, but my spirit feels thin,
Too busy saying yes to let myself in.
I've smiled through moments that didn't feel right,
And called it "being kind" while abandoning my fight.

But here's to the pause – a courageous new start,
A fence round the garden I grow in my heart.
If life hands me chaos and too much to do,
I'll answer with grace... and a well-placed "no," too.

Forget being everything, stretched to excess;
The art of my freedom begins with "no" – not "yes."

Contents

Introduction

THE ROOM IS FULL of noise – the steady hum of conversation, the light clink of glasses, the kind of laughter that should feel easy. But inside, there is that familiar tug. A tightening in the chest that grows every time a new request finds its way to you - as they inevitably do these days.

“What are your plans on Thursday?" "Can you take this on?" "Could you help out just for this weekend?"

Each request feels like a small withdrawal from an already-empty bank account. You nod. You smile. And you say yes. Even when something deep inside you is quietly whispering, 'No, no, please no.'

We tend to think of this as a personal flaw, but it’s a weight so many of us carry. For years, we’ve been the ones who show up, the ones who hold it all together. And somewhere along the way, that generosity starts to wear you down.

These pages are an invitation to change that. I’m not here to give you a rigid set of rules or a clinical lecture. I’m here to sit with you as we explore what it looks like to reclaim your own life. Setting a boundary is often called an act of courage, but really, it’s just an act of honesty.

It's about finally choosing to look after yourself with the same devotion you give to everyone else.

If you are a woman in the middle of your life – perhaps in that 30-to-60 stretch, or like me, closer to 70, where the world seems to ask the most of you – you know how heavy the "shoulds" can feel. Society, family, and work all have their expectations. It can feel almost impossible to put yourself first. But I want you to know it isn't just possible. It is necessary.

I've spent many years walking this path, both in my own life, as the eldest of four girls, and alongside women who have shared their stories with me. What we're doing here is blending a little bit of psychology with a lot of real-life practice. You'll find stories that might sound like your own and tools that feel like a deep breath.

We'll start by simply noticing why we feel we need to say yes in the first place. We'll look at what happens to our spirit when we don't have limits, and then we will move, slowly and kindly, toward saying no with conviction. We aren't building walls to keep people out; we're building bridges to more honest relationships.

I know the fears likely sitting with you right now; I have lived them. The worry that you'll be seen as selfish. The anxiety that a relationship might break if you stop over-extending. Those feelings are real and valid. But you'll find that when you start to respect your own time and energy, the people who truly matter start to respect it, too. It wasn't weakness that kept you saying yes for so long. It was survival. But now, we're looking for something more than just getting by.

I hope you'll engage with the reflections and prompts I've included. This isn't meant to be a passive read. Think of it as a conversation between us – a partnership, if you like. I'm here to help you untangle the knots of guilt and obligation that have held you back for far too long.

So, take a breath. Let it out slowly.

This is the start of a new chapter. One where saying no isn't an ending, but a beginning. It's the door to the freedom and self-respect you've always deserved.

Welcome. I'm glad you're here.

The Space Between Us

THERE IS A SPECIFIC kind of quiet that follows a "yes" you didn't want to give in the first place.

It's not a peaceful quiet. It isn't the silence of a house after everyone has finally gone to sleep, or the stillness of a garden in the early morning. It's a heavy, hollow sort of silence. It sits in the pit of your stomach while you drive home, the steering wheel feeling like lead in your hands. It's the silence that follows you into the bedroom. At the same time, you lie in bed staring at the ceiling, mentally calculating how much sleep you'll get if you finish that extra report tonight. It's the sound of a door closing on your own precious needs, and the faint, bitter echo of your own knowing voice saying a word your heart didn't agree with.

This silence is often accompanied by a low-grade vibration of static – an irritating internal noise that keeps you from ever fully relaxing. It's the mental list that never ends, the "open tabs" in your brain that keep processing even when you're trying to rest. For many of us, this has become a permanent background hum, like the sound of that bloody refrigerator you've stopped noticing until it suddenly cuts out. We've become so used to the internal compromise – the "yes" that feels like a betrayal – that we've forgotten what it feels like to live in our own skin without that pressure. We've traded our peace for a quiet life, only to find that the life we've kept quiet isn't really ours at all. It belongs to requests, expectations, and "shoulds."

At the heart of the struggle to say no is a simple word that often feels quite complicated: **boundaries**.

When you first start thinking about setting them, it can feel a little uncomfortable. It's like trying on a new pair of shoes that haven't quite molded to your feet yet. You feel stiff, maybe a bit self-conscious. You wonder if everyone is looking at you, noticing the change in your "fit." You might even feel like an imposter, as if you're playing a part you haven't quite earned the right to perform. You might worry that the moment you say "no," the people you love will see a version of you they don't recognize, and you're not sure if they'll like her as much as the one who always said "yes."

But without those boundaries, life starts to feel like a whirlwind. You're pulled in every direction, and eventually, you lose your sense of where you end, and everyone else begins. You become a blurry version of yourself, a person defined by the requests of others rather than your own internal compass. When you don't know where your own edges are, it's impossible to stand your ground. You become a shape-shifter, adapting to every room you enter, every person you talk to, until the "original" you is buried under layers of accommodation. You are everywhere for everyone, which usually means you are nowhere for yourself.

Boundaries aren't about shutting people out. I want to be very clear about that from the beginning. They aren't cold, and they aren't unkind. They are the lines that protect your spirit. They give you room to breathe, to reflect, and to actually grow into the person you were meant to be. They are the difference between being a home with a sturdy front door and being a public park where anyone can wander through at 2:00 AM, leave their trash, and walk all over the grass you've worked so hard to grow.

When you have a sturdy door, you get to choose who comes in. You get to decide when the house is open for visitors and when it is time for rest and family. You decide which conversations are welcome in your kitchen and which ones need to stay on the porch. That doesn't make you a fortress; it makes you a steward of your own life. It allows you to invite people in with a whole heart, rather than a resentful one. It means that when you *do* open the door, you are actually happy to see the person on the other side.

The Somatic Map: How Your Body Holds the "Yes"

Before we look at the psychology or the "why" behind our behavior, I want us to look at how it feels. Not in your head – we spend far too much time in our heads, rationalizing and overthinking – but in your body.

Most of us have become experts at ignoring our physical cues. We've been trained to "push through" and "keep going," as if our bodies are just inconvenient machines meant to carry our brains from one meeting to the next. But your body is a much more honest witness than your mind. Your mind can rationalize almost anything. It can justify a commitment by saying, *It's only an hour; she really needs the help; it would be rude to decline.* But your body doesn't deal in excuses or social niceties. Your body deals in the raw truth of your nervous system.

Overcommitment is rarely a sudden crash. It is a slow, quiet accumulation of small "yeses" that eventually leave you heavy. You might notice it first in your shoulders – that subtle lifting toward your ears that you don't even realize you're doing until you finally exhale at the end of the day and feel the sharp ache. Or perhaps it's a tightness in your jaw, a clenching that happens every time your phone buzzes with a new notification. Some women describe a "knot" in their stomach that only loosens when they are completely alone. Others feel a fluttering in their chest, a phantom anxiety that has no specific cause other than the weight of being "available" 24 hours a day.

Have you ever noticed that when someone asks you for a favor you don't want to do, your breath hitches? Just a tiny, sharp catch in the back of your throat. That is your nervous system telling you that your boundaries are being tested. It is the "freeze" response in miniature. Your body is saying *no* before your brain has even finished processing the request. If you start to pay attention, you'll find that your body has a "No" long before your mouth finds the "Yes." Learning to trust that physical flinch – that internal pulling back – is the beginning of self-respect. It is the body's way of saying, *We are full. We cannot take on any more.*

When we ignore these signals day after day, year after year, it leads to a chronic state of "wearing thin." It's not always a dramatic burnout where you can't get out of bed. Sometimes it's just a slow fading of your color. You feel it as a constant fatigue that sleep doesn't seem to touch. It's the kind of tired that lives in your bones. This exhaustion is as much about emotional labor as it is about physical effort. It's the exhaustion of performing a version of yourself that is always "on," always pleasant, and always available.

Think about the irritability that flares up over small things. The sound of the dishwasher being loaded incorrectly, the way your partner breathes while they're reading, a red light when you're already five minutes behind. This irritability isn't a character flaw. It isn't that you're becoming a "difficult" or "angry" person. It's a flare sent up by an overtaxed system. It's your spirit saying, *I have nothing left to give, yet the world keeps asking.* When your internal cup is empty, every drop you're asked for feels like an assault. We become "brittle" – prone to snapping because we are under too much tension.

And then there is resentment. Resentment is one of the most useful emotions we have, though we're often told to suppress it because it isn't "nice." But resentment is a signpost. It points directly to where a boundary has been crossed or where one was never set in the first place. When you feel that bitter edge creeping into your voice, or that hot flash of anger when a friend asks for "just five minutes" of your time, it's worth pausing. Ask yourself: *Where did I say yes when I meant no?* That resentment is the voice of the self you've ignored, finally trying to get your attention. It is the part of you that still loves yourself enough to be angry. It is your soul's way of protesting its own disappearance.

The "Good Girl" and the Ancestry of Compliance

To understand why it's so hard to say no now, we have to look back at where the habit started. None of us arrived at this place by accident. We were carefully, and often lovingly, trained to be this way. It is a legacy that goes back generations.

Most of us were raised to be "good girls." We learned early on that being helpful, quiet, and accommodating earned us praise and, more importantly, a sense of safety. We saw the smiles on our parents' faces when we were "easy" and didn't make demands. We saw the rewards at school for being the one who never caused trouble and always helped the teacher. We learned that a "yes" bought us belonging. We were taught that our value was tied to our utility – that we were loved for what we *did*, for how useful we could be, rather than for who we *were*.

We saw the women around us doing the same. Our mothers, grandmothers, and aunts were often the emotional glue of the family. They managed the household's moods – smoothing over conflicts, anticipating needs before they were even spoken, and setting their own desires on the back burner until the stove went cold. We saw them pride themselves on their self-sacrifice, as if being the most exhausted person in the room was a badge of honor. We didn't just learn this behavior; we inherited it like a family heirloom, passed down through generations of women who survived by being indispensable. We were told that being a "good woman" meant being a "selfless" one.

In that world, the ones who could always be counted on were the ones who were most valuable. But there is a high price for that kind of value. When you are the one who "holds it all together," you eventually become the one who isn't allowed to fall apart. You become invisible in your own life because everyone assumes you're fine. After all, you're always smiling, and you're always saying yes. You become the reliable fixture, the person who doesn't need checking in on. And eventually, you start to feel the profound loneliness of that reliability. You are surrounded by people, but no one really sees the person underneath the performance.

For women in midlife – that stretch between 30 and 60 – this is often where the crisis hits. You've spent decades being the nurturer, the employee who never complains, the daughter who handles every family emergency. You've built a life that functions like a well-oiled machine, but suddenly, you realize you are the oil. You are the one being consumed to keep the gears turning for everyone else. You look at your to-do list and realize your name isn't on it. Not even at the very bottom, after "buy milk" and "pick up dry cleaning."

This creates a slow erosion of identity. You look in the mirror, and you aren't sure who is looking back, because that person has spent so much time conforming to what others need that her own edges have blurred. You've become a mirror for everyone else's expectations, and you've forgotten what you look like when no one is watching. You might find yourself wondering: *What do I even like to eat when I'm not cooking for others? What would I do with an afternoon if no one needed anything from me?* The answers are often slow to come because the "you" who knows those answers has been in hiding for a long time. You have become a "stranger" to yourself.

I want you to know that it wasn't weakness that kept you in this cycle. It was a beautiful, albeit misplaced, desire for connection. You were doing what you were taught to do to stay loved. You were being the "anchor" because you were told the ship would drift away without you. But the connection you were maintaining was with everyone else, at the expense of the most important connection of all – the one with yourself. Now, we're just learning a different way to stay anchored – one that doesn't involve drowning so others can stay dry. We are learning that you can't be a bridge for others if you have no foundation of your own.

The Tightrope: Fear and the Shadow of Conflict

Fear is often the silent architect of our "yeses."

It rarely looks like a dramatic terror. Instead, it disguises itself as kindness, or "being a team player," or "being a good friend." But underneath those labels, it is often a primal fear of conflict or rejection. For many of us, the thought of disappointing someone feels like a threat to our sense of belonging. We imagine the look on their face – the slight furrow of the brow, the tightening of the mouth, the heavy silence that follows a "no" – and it feels like a personal failure. We interpret their disappointment as a sign of our own inadequacy. We feel "bad" because they feel "unhappy."

We walk a tightrope every day, trying to balance everyone's expectations, terrified that one "no" will cause us to fall. We worry that if we stop over-delivering, people will realize we aren't as essential as they thought we were. Or worse, that they'll decide we're "difficult" and start to withdraw their affection. We fear the "social tax" of being a woman with limits. We worry we'll be labeled "not a team player" at work, or "selfish" in our families, or "unreliable" in our friendships. This fear keeps us small, always checking the weather of other people's moods before we decide if it's safe to speak our truth.

But here is the truth we often miss: Avoidance creates its own stress. It is a debt we pay with our future peace.

When you say yes to avoid a difficult conversation, you aren't actually avoiding conflict. You're just moving the conflict inside. Instead of having a ten-minute uncomfortable talk with a friend or a colleague, you have a three-day argument with yourself. You punish yourself with guilt, exhaustion, and internal criticism just to spare someone else a moment of disappointment. You are effectively sacrificing your internal peace to maintain an external illusion of harmony. You are staying "nice" at the cost of being "kind" to yourself. And over time, that internal conflict becomes a weight that is much harder to carry than a few minutes of social awkwardness.

Courage isn't the absence of that fear. It's moving forward even when your hands are shaking a little. It's the realization that the world won't end if you stop being the one who makes everything okay for everyone else. It's understanding that other people's disappointment is theirs to manage – it isn't a debt you are required to pay.

I've found that mindfulness is a gentle way to start addressing this. It's not about sitting on a cushion for an hour; it's about just taking a single breath when a request comes in. That breath creates a small, sacred space between the "ask" and your "answer." In that space, the fear can still be there – it doesn't have to vanish – it doesn't have to be the one holding the pen. In that breath, you can notice the urge to please, the "fawn" response of your nervous system, and you can choose something else. You can choose to be honest.

In that space, you can ask yourself: *If I say yes to this, what am I saying no to in myself? Am I saying no to my sleep? My time with my children? My own peace of mind?* When you see it that way, a "yes" to someone else is always a "no" to something else in your own life. The question isn't whether you'll disappoint someone; it's *who* you are willing to disappoint. For a long time, the person you were most willing to disappoint was you. We're here to change that order. We're here to realize that disappointing yourself is the highest price of all.

The Weight of Legacy: Cultural and Generational Layers

We don't live in a vacuum. We carry the stories of the people who came before us, and sometimes those stories make saying "no" feel like a betrayal of our very history, our ancestors, and our identity.

In many cultures, the idea of a "personal boundary" is a foreign, almost offensive concept. If you come from a background that values the group, family, or community above all else, asserting your individual needs can feel like a deep act of rebellion. You might have been raised with the idea that self-sacrifice isn't just a choice – it's the highest form of virtue. To think of yourself was to be a "bad" member of the community, a "selfish" daughter, or a "disloyal" sister. The "we" always came before the "I."

Maybe you saw your grandmother work until her hands were calloused, never once asking for a thing for herself. In the light of her sacrifice, your desire for a quiet Sunday afternoon or the need to decline a family obligation might feel trivial, even shameful. You might feel the weight of generations of women who didn't have the luxury of saying no, and that weight can make your own voice feel very small. You feel like you owe it to them to keep going, to keep serving, as if your exhaustion is a tribute to their labor. You feel like saying "no" is a slap in the face to those who had no choice.

If you are balancing multiple cultural identities, perhaps navigating the expectations of a traditional family while working in a modern, individualistic environment, this tension is even sharper. You might value your independence and professional boundaries at work. Still, the moment you walk into your parents' home, you feel the old pressure to be the compliant, selfless daughter. It's a constant, exhausting code-switching. You are a different version of yourself depending on which language you are speaking or which house you are in. You are "modern" in one world and "traditional" in another, and neither version feels fully like *you*.

Navigating this takes a very soft touch. It isn't about rejecting your heritage or "breaking" with your culture. It's about finding a way to honor both your traditions and your own well-being. It's about realizing that you can be a "good daughter" or a "good friend" without being a hollowed-out one. You can respect the group while still honoring the individual who is part of it. You can love your family and still need time away from them to be a healthy version of yourself.

I remember talking to a woman named Maya who felt she couldn't say no to her mother's daily phone calls, even though they left her feeling drained and anxious long after the call ended. Her mother would talk for hours about the family's problems, and Maya felt it was her cultural duty to listen. She needed to work on finding a middle path. Maya didn't stop calling her mother, but she began to set a "container" for the calls. She started to say, "Mom, I love talking to you, but I only have fifteen minutes today before I need to focus on my rest so I can be ready for tomorrow."

At first, it was hard. Maya felt the old guilt – the ghost of her grandmother's voice whispering about duty and respect. But over time, she realized she was actually a better daughter when she wasn't listening with a heart full of resentment. She was more present for those fifteen minutes than she had been for the two hours of forced listening. She was still honoring her mother, but she was starting to honor herself, too. She was learning that love and limits can live in the same house. She was redefining what it meant to be "loyal."

The Myth of Selfishness

The word "selfish" is often used as a weapon against women who start to set boundaries. It's a way of pulling us back into the "good girl" mold. It is the label we fear most because it strikes at the heart of our identity as "givers." We have been taught that "giving" is our only worth, so "not giving" feels like losing our value entirely.

But we need to look at what that word actually means. Is it selfish to need rest? Is it selfish to protect your mental health so you don't snap at the people you love? Is it selfish to have a life that isn't entirely at the service of others? If a house has a fence, we don't call the owner selfish; we say they are taking care of their property. If a gardener fences off a section of the garden to let the soil recover, we call them wise. Why do we think of our time and energy any differently? Why do we treat our own spirit like common land that everyone is allowed to graze upon until it's a dustbowl?

If we don't have boundaries, we aren't actually giving from a place of love. We are giving from a place of obligation, fear, and eventually, exhaustion. That's not a gift; it's a transaction. You're "buying" approval with your energy. You're giving because you're afraid of what will happen if you *don't* give - fear of anger, fear of being disliked, fear of being alone. And eventually, that "giving" starts to taste like ash. The people you love aren't getting the best of you; they're getting the leftovers of a person who is starving for her own time and space.

When you set a boundary, you are actually making your relationships cleaner and more honest. You are saying, *I want to be with you because I choose to be, not because I'm afraid to say no.* That is a much more honest and sustainable way to live. It allows for true intimacy, because intimacy requires two whole people, not one person and one person-shaped shell. When you are honest about your needs, you give others permission to be honest about theirs. You create a relationship based on reality, not on a performance. You move from "people-pleasing" to "people-honoring."

Reframing "selfishness" as "integrity" changes everything. Integrity means your outside matches your inside. If you feel a "no" in your heart but say a "yes" with your lips, you are out of integrity with yourself. You are lying. And that lack of integrity is what causes that hollow, heavy feeling. When you are honest about your limits, you allow others to be honest about theirs, too. You create a space where everyone is allowed to be human, with human limits. You stop trying to be a saint or a superhero and start trying to be a woman who respects herself.

Self-care isn't a luxury. It isn't just about bubble baths or expensive retreats, though those can be lovely. It is the foundation that allows you to be truly present for what actually matters. You cannot pour from an empty cup, no matter how much you wish you could. Stewardship of your own energy is the kindest thing you can do for the people around you. It ensures that when you *do* say yes, you can mean it with every fiber of your being. It means that your "yes" has the weight of your whole heart behind it.

The First Seeds: Practicing in the Low Stakes

You don't start training for a marathon by running twenty-six miles. You start by walking around the block. And then you walk two. You build the muscle slowly, with patience and grace.

Setting boundaries is a muscle. If you haven't used it in forty years, it's going to be weak. It's going to feel shaky. It's going to ache the next day. That's okay. That is just the feeling of growth. Don't expect yourself to set a major boundary with your most difficult family member or your boss on day one. Start where the stakes are low and the air is clear. Start where the "no" won't feel like an earthquake.

I invite you to start practicing in the "low stakes" areas of your life. These are the moments where the consequences of a "no" are minimal, but the internal victory is significant. Each small "no" is a rehearsal for the bigger ones. It's like clearing a small path in a forest before you try to build a road.

Maybe it's telling the cashier you don't want to sign up for the rewards card today. Maybe it's letting a phone call go to voicemail when you're in the middle of your dinner or a book, instead of jumping to answer it out of habit. Maybe it's telling a friend you can't meet for coffee this week – not because you're "so busy" (the classic excuse), but because you just need the time to yourself. Notice how it feels to say no without having a "good enough" excuse to back it up. Notice the urge to lie and say you have an appointment, just to make the "no" more palatable for them. Practice staying with the simple truth: "I'm just not up for it this week, but thank you for asking."

Notice the urge to over-explain. When we provide a list of excuses, we are actually asking for permission. We're saying, *"Here are all my reasons; do you agree they are valid enough for me to say no?"* When we over-explain, we hand the power back to the other person, letting them decide if our fatigue is "real" enough to justify a refusal. Try just saying: "I can't do that this time, but thank you for thinking of me." You don't owe the world an itemized list of your exhaustion. Your time is yours by right, not by permission from others.

See what happens in your body when you say it. Notice the rush of adrenaline – that little spike of "Oh no, I said it!" – and then, if you can wait for it to pass, notice the quiet sense of relief that follows. You are starting to take up space in your own life. You are starting to draw the lines of your own map. You'll find that the world doesn't crumble. The cashier doesn't hate you. Your friend is still your friend. And you? You have a little more energy for the things that actually matter to you. You are reclaiming the "territory" of your own life, one small "no" at a time.

The Vision of Wholeness

As we move through this book, I want you to keep a vision in your mind. Not a vision of a "perfect" life where you never feel stressed, but a vision of a "whole" one.

Imagine a life where your "yes" has weight because people know it isn't guaranteed. Imagine waking up and knowing that your day belongs to you – not that you won't help others, but that you will do so from a place of choice and abundance, not depletion. Imagine the freedom of not having to scan every room you enter for "needs" you are expected to fill. Imagine the lightness of not being the "emotional custodian" for everyone in your life.

Imagine a version of yourself that is grounded and steady. A woman who knows her worth isn't tied to her productivity or her utility to others. A woman who can look at a conflict and not feel like the world is ending, but rather that an honest conversation is beginning. Imagine being someone who can be disappointed by others without feeling she has to "fix" their mood, and who can disappoint others without feeling she has "failed" as a person. Imagine the peace of no longer needing everyone's approval to feel okay.

It doesn't happen all at once. It's a slow, quiet turning of the tide. For a long time, the tide has been going out, leaving you dry and exposed. Now, we're inviting it back in. You've been a "performer" for a long time, making sure everyone else is comfortable while you sit in the wings, waiting for your own life to start. It's time to step out. Not to be the star, not to make a scene, but just to be the person who lives there. To be the woman who occupies the center of her own life.

You aren't being difficult. You're being honest. You are finally showing up for the most important relationship you will ever have – the one with the woman who has been waiting for you to notice her, to protect her, and to love her. She's been there all along, underneath the "yeses."

And that is more than enough.

The Shift Within

Unlearning the Myth of "Selfish"

You wake up, and before your feet even hit the floor, the weight of the day is already there. It isn't your own weight, though. It's the stack of "yeses" you've given to everyone else - the volunteer committee you don't have time for, the extra project at work you took on to prove your worth. This friend always needs a listener but never seems to notice when you're the one struggling. It's the mental list of who needs what, when they need it, and how you're going to squeeze the small, tired remains of yourself into the narrow gaps left over.

Somewhere along the way, we were taught that being a good woman meant being an empty one. We were raised on a specific narrative of the "selfless nurturer" - the one who keeps the fire burning for everyone else, even if she has to use her own floorboards for kindling. We were taught that having boundaries meant being a disappointment, and that prioritizing our own peace was a betrayal of our very nature. We learned to apologize for our needs before we even finished stating them.

We call it selfishness. But really, it's just survival.

When we look back at how we were shaped, we see that female identity was often tightly bound to service.

A woman who stood her ground, prioritized her rest, or simply said "not today" was seen as neglecting her "duty." These labels have seeped into the fibers of our being, becoming a voice in our heads that whispers, 'Who do you think you are?' every time we try to take a seat before the work is "done." But in midlife, we begin to realize a hard truth: the work is never truly done, and the chair is the only thing keeping us upright. If we wait until every task is finished and every person is satisfied before we rest, we will never sit down.

When you look at the people who truly sustain others - the leaders who inspire, the mothers who actually enjoy their children, the friends who stay the course for decades - they aren't the ones running on empty. They are the ones who have learned that self-preservation isn't a luxury. It's the price of admission for a meaningful life. It's about stewardship. If you were given a fine, rare instrument to play, you wouldn't leave it out in the rain or let the strings snap from neglect. You are that instrument. If you are out of tune or broken, the music stops for everyone.

It's the old airplane metaphor: put your mask on first. It's a cliché because it's true. You cannot breathe for someone else if you are gasping for air yourself. Helping others from a place of depletion isn't a gift; it's an unsustainable debt. When we give from an empty cup, we aren't giving love; we are giving resentment, disguised as kindness. We are giving a "yes" that tastes like vinegar. Eventually, the bill comes due, usually in the form of a snap at a loved one who didn't deserve it, a sudden illness that forces us to stop, or a quiet, crushing sense of bitterness that colors our entire world.

The evidence is there, too, if you need it. When we stop the constant output, our nervous systems finally get a chance to settle. The frantic "fight or flight" response - that low-level hum of anxiety that defines so many of our days - begins to quiet down. Stress hormones like cortisol recede. Clarity returns. You aren't just "nicer" to be around; you are more present. You are more you.

A Moment for Reflection: Redefining the Word

Think back to the last time you felt a pang of guilt for saying no or taking an hour for yourself.

· What did that guilt actually feel like in your body? Was it a tightness in the throat? A heaviness in the pit of your stomach? Did it feel like a physical weight pulling your shoulders down? Notice how your body reacts to the idea of being "selfish."

· Who told you that your time wasn't yours to keep? Was it a parent, a boss, or a societal ghost you've never actually met, yet whose approval you still crave? Often, we are trying to satisfy voices that aren't even in the room anymore.

Try to look at that moment again through a different lens. Instead of "selfish," call it "maintenance." You were taking care of the only tool you have to navigate this world: yourself. It wasn't an act of theft from others; it was an act of radical honesty toward yourself.

Self-Care as a Quiet Necessity

In a world that rewards burnout, exhaustion has become a status symbol. We wear our "busy-ness" like a badge of honor, a sign that we are important, productive, and desperately needed. We compare calendars like warriors compare scars, almost as if the person with the least sleep wins. But underneath the badge, the threads are fraying. The constant buzz of notifications, the pressure to "do it all" with a smile, and the blurred lines of a digital life mean we are never truly "off." Even our sleep is often just a shallow, fitful pause in the performance.

And somewhere along the way, that performance starts to wear you down. It starts with a lack of patience, then a lack of joy, and finally, a lack of self.

There is a vital difference between indulgence and essential self-care. Indulgence is an escape - it's the impulse buy, the mindless scrolling, or the weekend away to forget your life exists. It's a temporary numbing. Essential self-care is the work you do so you don't *have* to escape your life. It is foundational. It's the quiet, often boring choices that sustain your health and your spirit daily. It isn't always pretty, and it rarely makes for a good social media post. It's the unglamorous work of being your own guardian.

It is the choice to go to bed early, even when the kitchen is still messy, and the emails are still unread. It's the glass of water when you'd rather have another coffee to push through the fatigue. It's the ten minutes of sitting in the driveway in silence after work, letting the "professional self" dissolve before the "home self" takes over. These aren't treats you earn by working hard; they are the scaffolding that holds the entire structure of your life together. Without them, the building eventually collapses, no matter how beautiful the facade.

If your life feels too crowded for a reset, start small. We don't need to add a daunting new hour to our day; we just need to reclaim the minutes we are already losing to the void. Use "habit stacking." Pair a moment of mindfulness with something you already do every single day. While the coffee brews, just breathe. Don't check your phone. Don't check the news, the weather, or the calendar. Just feel the floor under your feet and the air in your lungs. These tiny windows of time aren't much on their own, but they accumulate like interest. They remind you that you are a person, not a productivity machine.

The Daily Reset

What are three things that make you feel like yourself again? Not what you *should* do, but what actually settles your spirit.

· A walk without a podcast, a phone, or a destination - just listening to the rhythm of your own feet on the pavement and noticing the color of the sky.

· Sitting with a cup of tea until it's actually gone, watching the steam rise without picking up a book or a device. Just being with the warmth.

· Take three deep, intentional breaths the moment the inbox feels like it's closing in on you. Feel your ribcage expand, and your shoulders drop.

Keep these resets close. They are your anchors in the storm of the everyday. They are small, private declarations of independence from a world that wants all of you.

The Steady Power of Assertiveness

There is a specific kind of fear that comes when someone asks for "one more thing." You feel the "no" in your chest - a cold, clear realization that you simply cannot do it - but the "yes" comes out of your mouth before you can stop it. You want to set a limit, but the word gets stuck in your throat because you're afraid of the friction it might cause. You're afraid of being labeled as "difficult," "unhelpful," or "not a team player."

Assertiveness isn't about being loud or aggressive. It's not about bulldozing people or "winning" an argument. It's just the steady middle ground between disappearing (passivity) and attacking (aggression). It's having a voice that doesn't need to shout to be heard. It is the art of standing in your own space without apologizing for occupying it. It says what is true, without malice or hesitation.

In the office, it looks like saying: *"I see why this project matters, but my plate is currently full. If I take this on, the quality of my other work will suffer. Let's look at the priorities together and see what can be moved."* At home, it looks like: *"I value our time together, but I am at my limit today. I need an hour of quiet right now so I can be fully present with you later."*

It feels clunky and terrifying at first. You might feel like you're being "cold." You might have to sit in the awkward silence that follows a "no" without rushing in to fill it with excuses or apologies. But that silence is where your respect for yourself lives. Honesty is actually the highest form of respect you can give someone else, too. When you say "yes" when you mean "no," you are lying to them. You are offering a version of yourself that doesn't exist. Eventually, they will feel the weight of that lie in your irritability or your absence. When you set a boundary, you're telling the truth about what you can give, which allows for a connection that is real rather than performed.

Over time, something happens. People stop expecting you to be the "yes" person. They start to respect your time because *you* respect your time. It shifts the dynamic from service to mutual respect. You stop being a resource to be used and start being a person to be engaged with.

Releasing the Need for Applause

Many of us grew up believing our worth was a moving target. If we got the grades, the praise, or the "likes," we were okay. We were the "good girls," the reliable ones, the ones who never caused a stir and always anticipated everyone else's needs. But when you live for external validation, you're building your house on sand. The tide comes in, the opinions shift, and suddenly you don't know who you are without the applause. You become a chameleon, constantly changing colors to match the expectations of whatever room you're in, until you can no longer remember your original shade.

Internal validation is the slow, quiet, and often lonely work of becoming your own home.

It starts with small affirmations - not the "perfect" kind you see on inspirational posters, but quiet, gritty truths spoken in the dark. *"I am allowed to be tired." "My worth is not tied to my to-do list." "I don't need to prove I'm busy to prove I'm valuable."* When we stop looking outside for permission to exist, something shifts in our posture. We start to make choices based on our own inner compass rather than someone else's map. We stop asking "is this what they want?" and start asking "is this what I need?"

This shift has consequences. Let's be honest: some people in your life may be frustrated when you stop performing for them. They liked the version of you that never said no. They found it convenient. But the people who truly love you will stay, and they will eventually enjoy the version of you that is actually happy and rested, not just compliant. It's a series of small, private victories where you choose your own peace over someone else's approval. Eventually, the only opinion that holds real, lasting weight is the one you see in the mirror at the end of the day.

The Relief of Being Real

Authentic communication is like a cool breeze on a sweltering day. There is such a deep, physical relief in finally dropping the mask. We spend so much energy performing - trying to be the perfect employee, the "strong" partner, the friend who never complains. This performance is exhausting; it's like carrying an extra suitcase everywhere you go, filled with all the things you think you're supposed to be.

But people can tell when you're being real. They can feel the difference between a rehearsed "I'm fine" and a sincere "I'm having a hard week, but I'm hanging in there." Sincerity creates a space where others feel safe to be real, too. It's an invitation for them to put down their own suitcases and just be.

It takes courage to be vulnerable, especially in environments where we feel we have to be "on." You don't have to share everything with everyone - authenticity isn't oversharing; it's integrity. It's ensuring that what you say on the outside matches the truth of what you feel on the inside. It's about being whole rather than fragmented, letting your "yes" be "yes" and your "no" be "no."

At work, you can say, *"I'm struggling to see the path forward on this; let's talk it through."* In your family, you can say, *"I'm feeling a bit overwhelmed by the noise right now, I need ten minutes of quiet before we start dinner."*

This transparency builds more trust than "perfect" ever could. It makes you human. And humans are much easier to love and much more effective to work with than icons of perfection. When we are real, we stop being a role and start being a soul.

Resilience: Learning to Gather the Pieces

Resilience isn't about being unbreakable. It's not about being a "warrior" who never falls or a stone that never cracks under pressure. It's about how you gather the pieces after you've been broken. It's the art of the mend - recognizing that the cracks don't make you less valuable; they just show where you've been.

Think of it as a growth mindset. It's the ability to look at a setback - a failed project, a strained relationship, a personal mistake - and ask, *"What is this trying to show me?"* rather than *"What is wrong with me?"* It's the understanding that a "failure" is just data. It's information you can use for the next step. If you view life as a series of experiments rather than a series of final tests, the fear of failing starts to lose its grip. You become more curious and less afraid.

We see resilience in the world all the time - in the woman starting over after a loss, in the person trying again after a long silence. But you see it in yourself, too, if you look closely enough. Every time you've navigated a day that felt impossible, every time you've stood back up after being knocked down by life's surprises, you were building resilience. It's the quiet strength that says, *I am still here, and I am still learning.*

It isn't a gift; some people are born with it, while others are left wanting. It's a muscle that gets stronger every time life asks you to flex it. You build it through gratitude - not the "toxic positivity" kind that ignores pain, but the kind that acknowledges that even in the dark, there is still breath in your lungs and beauty to be found in the small things. You build it through mindfulness, staying in the present moment when the future feels too big and the past feels too heavy. You build it by being kind to yourself when things go wrong.

As we move forward, hold onto this: your needs are valid. You aren't a project to be fixed or a problem to be solved; you are a person to be cared for. Taking care of yourself isn't just permissible - it's the most honest, courageous thing you can do for yourself and for everyone who relies on you.

As we wrap up this chapter on the mind, remember that emotional resilience is not merely about survival; it is about thriving in the midst of change. It involves identifying and capitalizing on growth opportunities, even amid formidable circumstances. In our ensuing chapter, we will delve into the practical strategies of setting boundaries - the physical and verbal manifestation of the mindset we have built here. We will move from the *why* to the *how*.

Finding the Words

Your Personal Boundary Statements

Your phone buzzes on a Tuesday evening. It's that exact moment you've finally sat down, the house is beginning to settle, and you've just taken your first deep breath of the day. It's another request - a small favor from a neighbor who needs a ride, a weekend shift "just this once" to cover a colleague, or perhaps an invitation to a school committee you simply don't have the heart for anymore. You're already juggling a dozen glass balls, and here is one more being tossed your way, expected to be caught with a full heart and a practiced smile.

You feel that familiar tightening in your chest. Maybe a slight heat in your neck, a sudden, shallow catch in your breath, or that dull ache in the pit of your stomach that you've learned to live with. It's a low-grade vibration of "not again."

That physical reaction isn't an inconvenience to be ignored or pushed down; it's a messenger. It's your body's way of telling you that you've reached your edge before your mind has even had the chance to process the request. For so many of us, we've spent the better part of two or three decades ignoring that heat, pushing past the tightness until it just becomes a dull, constant background noise - the low-grade hum of chronic overextension that we mistake for "normal" adulthood.

We've been conditioned to think that being "available" is the same as being "good," and that being "tired" is just the price of admission for a meaningful life. We have become experts at reading everyone else's needs while becoming strangers to our own.

Finding your voice in these moments isn't about building a cold, grey wall to keep the world at bay; it's about drawing a soft, clear circle around what matters so you can actually show up for the people and the work inside that circle. A wall isolates you, but a circle protects what is sacred. It starts with having a few simple sentences ready - words that feel like yours, not scripts borrowed from a corporate manual. When you say, *"I'm not available for extra work this weekend,"* or *"I need this evening to recharge,"* you aren't just giving an answer to someone else. You're coming home to yourself. You're deciding that your peace is a precious resource worth protecting, not a bottomless well for others to draw from whenever they feel a thirst.

It doesn't happen all at once.

We often spend the first half of our lives being praised for how much we can carry. We were the "good" daughters, the "reliable" employees, the "strong" friends who never missed a beat, even when we were crumbling inside. We wore our exhaustion like a badge of honor, unaware of the compounding cost until we find ourselves in midlife, looking in the mirror and wondering where the "real" us went. Breaking that cycle requires us to sit with the deep, vibrating discomfort of being the one who, for once, says no. It feels like a betrayal of our training, but it is actually a reclamation of our life.

It wasn't weakness that kept you saying yes. It was survival.

At first, we need clarity. Not the clinical, list-making kind, but a quiet honesty about what we can actually carry without breaking. This is a seasonal audit. What you could carry at thirty might be too heavy at fifty, and that is not a failure - it is a fact of nature. Our capacity shifts as our seasons change. We have less patience for the performative and a greater hunger for the essential. When we know our "why" - the Saturday morning coffee in a quiet house, the hobby we've finally picked back up after twenty years, or simply the mental health we are desperately trying to preserve - the "no" becomes much steadier. It isn't about being rigid or difficult. It's about being faithful to your own capacity.

The Language of "No"

Sometimes it helps to have a starting point because, in the heat of the moment, our brains tend to default to "yes" just to stop the immediate spike of anxiety. We want the pressure to go away, so we agree to the bake sale or the extra project, only to feel the heavy, familiar weight of resentment settle in just moments after the conversation ends. Resentment is usually a sign that a boundary has been crossed, or that we failed to set one in the first place.

If a friend asks you to go somewhere when you are bone-tired, you might say: *"I appreciate you thinking of me, but I'm going to pass so I can focus on some things at home."*

It is simple. It is clear. It doesn't require a long story to justify it.

You say yes to others. Even when something in you says no.

We often feel the need to explain *why* we are saying no, as if we're presenting a case to a judge and jury. We list our symptoms, our chores, our commitments, hoping the other person will "allow" us to stay home. We over-explain because we feel guilty for having needs. But "I can't make it" is a full sentence. You don't need to mention the laundry, the headache, or the long day at work. Those are your private reasons, and you are allowed to keep them.

When we offer too many excuses, we accidentally invite the other person to help us "solve" our problems so we can eventually say yes. We turn our boundary into a negotiation, and in a negotiation, the person with the most persistence usually wins. If we say, "I can't come because I have too much laundry," we are inviting them to say, "Oh, just leave the laundry for tomorrow!"

Learning to flip that script takes practice. The words might feel clunky at first. They might stick in your throat like a secret you aren't supposed to tell. That's okay. Try saying them out loud while you're making tea or driving alone. It's not about being a performer; it's about getting used to the sound of your own limits.

There is also power in the pause. In our digital age, the ping of a notification often feels like a demand for an immediate answer. But you don't have to answer the text the second it arrives. You don't have to answer the question the moment it's asked. If your "fawn" response

- that instinct to please and appease - is strong, give yourself a buffer. Try: *"Let me check my calendar and get back to you."* This isn't a lie; your "calendar" includes your mental space, your energy levels, and your soul's need for quiet. Even five minutes of space allows the nervous system to settle. It gives adrenaline a chance to recede, allowing you to respond from a place of truth rather than panic.

A Moment for Reflection

Think of three times lately when you wanted to say no but didn't. Don't judge yourself for it; just look at it with a gentle curiosity. What stopped you? Was it a fear of disappointing them, or a fear of what they would think of you? Often, we find that the people who truly love us actually want us to be honest. They don't want the "ghost" of us at their party; they want the real us, even if that means we can't come today. What would those versions of you have liked to say if they felt safe? Write those sentences down now. Keep them somewhere close - not as a "to-do" list, but as a reminder that your time is yours to give, not theirs to take.

At the Desk: Professional Limits

Work often feels like the hardest place to draw these lines. In midlife, we often find ourselves at a crossroads of responsibility - managing others, or perhaps being the most experienced person in the room. We carry the "invisible load" of knowing how things work and where the mistakes are buried. We worry that if we stop saying yes, we'll be seen as less capable, less committed, or perhaps replaceable by someone younger and "hungrier."

This is the "competence trap" - being so good at handling things that everyone assumes you can handle *everything*. It is the reward for being reliable: more work.

But there is a quiet integrity in doing a few things well rather than many things poorly. When you are spread too thin, you're not actually helping the company; you're just increasing the likelihood of mistakes. You become a bottleneck rather than a resource. You lose the ability to see the big picture because you are too busy drowning in the details of everyone else's tasks.

It wasn't weakness that made you take on too much in the past. It was survival. You were building a career, providing for a family, or proving your worth in a world that often measures people by their output.

But now, we're looking for sustainability. We're looking for a way to work that doesn't leave us hollowed out by Friday afternoon, unable to enjoy the very life we're working so hard to build. Instead of a sharp *"I can't,"* which can feel jarring in a professional setting, try: *"To make sure I give my current projects the attention they need, I won't be taking on anything new right now."* This reframes your "no" as a commitment to quality. It shows that you value the work enough to protect it from your own exhaustion.

Or, if a manager adds to your plate when you're already at capacity: *"I'm happy to help with this, but which of my current tasks should I deprioritize to make room for it?"* This forces the other person to recognize your humanity and the finite nature of time. It isn't a sign of slowing down; it's a sign of professional respect - for the work, and for yourself. When we stop running on empty, the quality of what we do changes. We become more present. We become more effective anchors for our teams. And slowly, the culture around us starts to adjust to the space we've claimed. You might even find that by setting your own boundaries, you give your colleagues the "permission" they've been waiting for to set their own.

At the Table: Family and History

Family is different. These boundaries are wrapped in decades of tradition, shared history, and the quiet, often unspoken weight of expectation. The kitchen table has a long memory. You might be playing a role that was cast for you thirty years ago - the peacekeeper who smooths things over, the organizer who handles the holidays, or the "strong" one who handles the difficult relatives so no one else has to. We often fear that if we stop playing the role, the whole play will fall apart.

But sometimes, the play needs to fall apart so a better, more honest one can begin.

In these spaces, it's often helpful to lead with warmth so the "no" doesn't feel like a rejection of the person or the bond. *"I love our Sunday dinners, but I'm going to stay home this week to rest. I'll see you all next time."* It's a soft reframe. You aren't rejecting the family; you are honoring a need for quiet. You are teaching them that you are a person with needs, not just a function of the family unit.

We often carry the "silent scripts" of the women who came before us - mothers and grandmothers who perhaps never had the luxury or the language to say no. They gave until they were transparent, and we watched them do it. We saw them sigh as they washed the dishes at midnight, or heard the sharpness in their voice that came from decades of unmet needs. Breaking those generational patterns is heavy, sacred work. It might cause a few ripples. People might be confused, or even a little annoyed, when the person who always says "yes" starts to say "maybe" or "not today."

This is particularly true for the "sandwich generation" - those of us caring for aging parents while still guiding our own children. The demands are relentless. You are being pulled in two directions by people you love deeply, and it is easy to forget that you are the one holding it all together. If you don't set boundaries here, you will disappear into the cracks of everyone else's needs. You cannot pour from an empty cup, but more importantly, you shouldn't have to be a cup that is constantly being emptied.

Consistency is your friend. Families thrive on what they can predict. When you consistently honor your limits with kindness, people eventually stop trying to negotiate them. They learn that your "no" is not an invitation to debate or a guilt trip; it is simply a fact of your existence. It takes time. Be patient with them, and with yourself.

In the World: Social Grace

Social invites can feel like a flurry of obligations, especially in an age where we are constantly "reachable" through half a dozen different apps. We feel the "shoulds" pulling at us, telling us that we need to be seen, to stay "relevant," or to be the life of the party. We worry that if we stop showing up to everything, the invites will stop coming altogether, and we'll be forgotten in the rush of life.

But an invitation is not a summons.

When you decline an invite because you're drained, you're choosing a different kind of connection - the one with yourself. A simple, *"Thanks for the invite, but I have other plans,"* is enough. Even if those "plans" are just sitting on your porch in the fading light, listening to the birds and letting the day wash off you. You are allowed to be your own best company.

We often suffer from a "social hangover" when we force ourselves to go out, out of guilt. We're there in body, but our spirit is elsewhere, wishing for the couch and a quiet room. We find ourselves checking the time or feeling irritable with people we usually love. That isn't being a good friend; it's being a ghost.

Choosing quality over quantity in our friendships doesn't make us lonely. It makes our "yes" mean so much more when we finally give it. When you show up, you do so fully, with your whole heart and undivided attention. That is a gift to your friends as much as it is to yourself. Real friends don't want you there if it's costing you your peace.

The Empathetic No

There is an art to saying no without closing your heart. This is perhaps the most important tool for the empathetic soul - those of us who feel the weight of everyone else's needs as if they were our own. We have a tendency to "over-identify" with other people's problems, taking them on as tasks to be solved. We think that by suffering alongside them, we are helping them. Still, we usually just double the suffering in the room.

When someone comes to you in need, and you truly have nothing left to give, acknowledge the bridge between you first. *"I can see you're going through a lot right now, and I wish I had the bandwidth to help. Right now, I just don't."* This is the empathetic no. It recognizes the other person's humanity without sacrificing your own. It acknowledges that while their problem is real and valid, it is not necessarily yours to solve at the expense of your own stability. Someone else's disappointment is not a fire you are required to put out.

Often, we find that when we don't jump in to "fix" everything, it gives the other person the space they need to find their own strength. We might actually be standing in the way of their growth by always being the safety net. By holding your boundary, you are inadvertently telling them that you believe they can handle their own journey. You are honoring their strength as much as your own.

The Boundary Hangover

After you say no - especially if it's the first time with a particular person - you might experience what I call the "boundary hangover." It's that wave of guilt, doubt, and anxiety that crashes over you the moment you hang up the phone or send the text. You'll wonder if you were too harsh. You'll worry they're mad. You'll be tempted to send a follow-up text to "fix" it or take it back. You might even find yourself replaying the conversation for hours, looking for ways you could have made it "nicer."

When this happens, just sit with it. Don't act on the anxiety. It's not a sign that you did something wrong; it's just the sound of an old habit trying to survive. Your nervous system is recalibrating. It has been tuned for "yes" for decades, and "no" feels like an alarm bell.

The guilt isn't the truth; it's just a feeling that belongs to a version of you that is ready to be retired. Let it pass through you like a weather system. It usually lasts about twenty minutes if you don't feed it with more overthinking. Make a cup of tea, walk to the window, or just breathe through the tightness. It will pass. And on the other side of that guilt is freedom.

Staying the Course

As we move forward, remember that boundaries are how we teach the world to love us. They are the quiet declarations of our worth. They don't isolate us; they allow us to show up authentically, without the low-grade bitterness that comes from being constantly over-extended and under-appreciated. Bitterness is the heavy price we pay for the boundaries we fail to set.

Think of your energy like a well. If you let other people take from your energy well whenever they please, soon there will be nothing but mud and gravel at the bottom. By protecting the water, you ensure there is always something clear and cool to offer when the time is truly right - when you decide to give from your overflow, not your essence.

It won't be perfect. You will likely say "yes" when you mean "no" at least once this week. You might feel that old familiar guilt creep in as you set your phone down. When that happens, don't beat yourself up. Don't add "failing at boundaries" to your list of stresses. Just notice it. Take a breath. Each time you notice, you are getting closer to the version of you that speaks her truth without apology. Each "no" to something that drains you is a silent "yes" to your own life.

Take a breath. You’re doing better than you think.

The Inner Work of Boundaries

The Feeling of Quiet Authority

Imagine a moment where someone asks you for something you simply cannot give - a Saturday afternoon commitment when you are bone-tired, a loan of emotional energy you don't have, or a task that pushes you past your physical limit. Usually, there is a noise that starts in the mind the moment they finish speaking. It's the noise of "should," the frantic search for a "good enough" excuse that they won't be able to argue with, and that jittery, child-like feeling of wanting to be liked at any cost. You might feel your heart rate climb or a sudden heat in your face, the physical manifestations of a "yes" that is already forming in your throat before your mind has even had a chance to say no.

You say yes. Even when something in you says no.

But this time, you just stay still. You let the request hang in the air for a second, resisting the urge to fill the silence. You decline, and you don't offer a flurry of justifications or a three-paragraph apology. You don't mention your busy schedule or your headache; you simply state your boundary. The world doesn't end. The person doesn't disappear into a cloud of smoke. You feel steady, like a tree with roots that go deeper than the surface-level wind. This stillness is your power. It is the realization that you don't need a "valid" reason to protect your peace; your need for peace is reason enough.

This is what happens when we let emotional intelligence do the heavy lifting. It isn't a clinical skill or a corporate theory to be memorized in a seminar; it's simply the hard-won ability to sit with your own feelings - and the feelings of the person across from you - without losing your footing. It's the compass that keeps you pointed toward home when the pressure starts to rise, and the "people-pleaser" in you wants to take the wheel. It's about being the adult in the room of your own mind, speaking to that anxious part of yourself with a voice that is calm, firm, and undeniably kind.

For many of us, "no" has always felt like a confrontation, or worse, a betrayal. We've been taught since we were small that being helpful is the same as being "good," and that being "good" is the only way to stay safe and loved. We learned to monitor the moods of adults and friends, adjusting our own shapes to fit their needs until we forgot what our original shape even was. But quiet authority comes when you realize that your "no" isn't an attack on them; it's a protection of your own center. It is the difference between being a performer who meets everyone's expectations and a woman who finally knows her own worth. When you speak from this place, you aren't trying to "win" the conversation or prove a point; you are simply stating a fact about your capacity, much as you would state the color of the sky.

We all have those moments where a small, simple request - like being asked to bring a dish to a potluck or stay ten minutes late - feels like the weight of the entire world. It usually isn't about the potluck. It's the cumulative stress of a month where you haven't sat down for a meal. It's an old fear of not being "enough" bubbling to the surface, reminding you of times you were criticized for not doing more. It's that sharp intake of breath when the phone vibrates, or the way your stomach drops before you've even read the email. These are signals from your body, not failures of your character. They are your nervous system's way of saying, *Wait. Something here is too much.* They are visceral reminders that you have been operating at a deficit for far too long.

When you start to recognize those triggers, they lose their power over you. You begin to see the storm before it breaks. You realize that your reaction isn't a sign of weakness; it's your system trying to tell you that something is out of balance. It's an invitation to pause, to breathe, and to remember that you are allowed to have a "too much" point. You begin to treat these feelings with curiosity rather than judgment. Instead of saying, "Why am I so stressed over nothing?" you say, "My body is feeling overwhelmed right now. What do I need to feel safe?"

And somewhere along the way, it starts to wear you down. Recognizing that weariness is the first step toward changing it.

It's also about noticing how others react. Some people will be fine with your "no." They might even respect you more for it, finding your clarity refreshing. Others might feel resentful or offer a sharp, passive-aggressive comment meant to make you feel small or guilty. They might say, "Oh, I thought you were someone I could count on," or simply fall into a heavy, pointed silence. By staying tuned in, you realize that their reaction is entirely theirs. It reflects their own needs, their own lack of boundaries, and their own history of being told they couldn't say no. You don't have to carry it. You are responsible for your delivery - making sure it is kind and clear - but you are not responsible for their reception. You can be the lighthouse that stays still while the waves crash against the base. The lighthouse doesn't move just because the sea is angry; it simply continues to shine.

The Foundation

At the heart of this work is a simple, unhurried kind of self-awareness. It's the quiet act of noticing how a conversation changes your breathing or tightens your shoulders. It's asking, "What am I feeling right now?" before you ever open your mouth to answer. Are you saying yes because you want to, or because you're afraid of the silence that follows a no? When you know your own limits, you stop reacting on impulse and start responding with intention. You learn to give yourself the gift of the "long pause" - that extra breath that allows your brain to catch up with your heart.

Then there is empathy.

We often think empathy means we have to give in because we understand why the other person is asking. We feel their stress, so we take it on as our own emotional backpack, thinking that by suffering alongside them, we are being "supportive." But it's possible to step into someone else's shoes and understand their disappointment while still keeping your own feet firmly on the ground. You can see their need without feeling responsible for fixing it. Empathy without boundaries is just self-destruction. It leads to a life where you are constantly leaking energy into everyone else's cup, leaving your own bone-dry.

It wasn't weakness that made you give so much for so long. It was survival. But now, you are learning a different way to be.

You can be kind and firm at the same time. These terms aren't opposites; they are partners. In fact, the kindest thing you can do for someone is to be honest with them about what you can actually sustain. A "yes" given out of resentment is a hollow gift. It leaves a bitter, metallic taste for everyone involved. You might be there in body, but your spirit is miles away, nursing a grudge. Over time, those hollow gifts build a wall of resentment that is much harder to break down than a simple, honest "no" would have been. True intimacy requires the truth, even when the truth is: *"I can't do that right now."* By being honest, you are inviting the other person into a real relationship rather than a performance.

This kind of growth isn't a race. It's a practice that happens in the small, unremarkable corners of your day - the way you handle a telemarketer, the way you tell a neighbor you can't chat right now, the way you choose to go to bed instead of answering one more text. It might just look like five minutes of quiet in the morning with your coffee, watching your thoughts move by like clouds without trying to fix them or judge them. Or it might be an honest conversation with a friend where you really listen, and they do the same - a space where neither of you is trying to "win" or "fix," but simply to be seen. These moments of connection build the muscle you'll need when the harder conversations come. They prove to your nervous system that it is safe to be seen as you are, limits and all.

The shift happens slowly. It's not a sudden, loud transformation but a gradual thinning of the internal noise. You might find that one day, you say no and the usual wave of guilt simply doesn't arrive. Or it arrives, but it feels smaller, more manageable. Soon, the misunderstandings start to fade, and the connections that remain feel more honest and less like a transaction. You stop apologizing for having a life that has edges and limits.

You begin to respect yourself enough to be truthful, and you find that the people who truly love you are relieved by your honesty - it gives them permission to be honest, too.

A Moment for Reflection

Think back to a time this week when saying "no" felt heavy. What was actually happening in your body? Did your chest tighten? Did your mind start rehearsing a long list of reasons why you "couldn't" do it, as if you were on trial? Just notice that pattern. You don't need to judge it or change it today. Just recognize the way your body tries to negotiate your boundaries for you. It is often just trying to keep you safe in the way it learned when you were much younger - perhaps when being "easy-going" was the only way to get through the day. Acknowledge that effort, then let it go. Tell that younger version of you: "I've got this now."

When the Music Changes

Setting a boundary is a bit like a dance. For years, you've followed a certain rhythm - the rhythm of being the one who always says yes, the one who handles the chaos, the one who smooths things over so no one else has to feel uncomfortable. Suddenly, you've decided to change the steps. It's natural for the people around you to stumble at first. They are still dancing to the old song, and they might feel clumsy, confused, or even offended that you aren't following the script anymore. This friction isn't a sign of failure; it's a sign that something real is happening.

Some might even get angry. Some might try to pull you back into the old dance by using guilt, or by telling you that you've "changed."

When someone reacts poorly to your boundary, it's often because of unmet needs or discomfort with change. They might have relied on your silence for a long time to keep their own lives comfortable and predictable. Their frustration isn't a sign that you did something wrong; it's a sign that the dynamic is shifting into something more honest. It isn't a reflection of your worth. It's just the friction that happens when things are being rearranged. Sometimes people have to let go of the version of you they were using to find the one that is actually there.

In those moments, your breath is your best friend. A slow inhale and an even slower exhale can be the shield that keeps you from being swept up in their chaos. You might find that your voice shakes the first few times you hold the line. That's okay. Let it shake. You are allowed to be nervous while being firm. Bravery isn't the absence of the shake; it's speaking through it. You might say something simple: *"I can see this is frustrating for you, but I need to stick to my decision for my own well-being."* You don't need to fill the silence that follows with more words or more apologies. You don't need to bargain. You don't need to apologize for the space you're taking up.

It doesn't happen all at once. It takes time for the new rhythm to feel natural.

It's like watching a summer storm from the safety of a porch. You can see the rain falling, you can hear the thunder, but you aren't getting wet. Their reaction is a passing cloud. It might feel loud and heavy in the moment, but it doesn't define the weather of your entire relationship unless you let it. Sometimes, the most loving thing you can do is let them have their reaction without trying to manage it for them. By not "fixing" their feelings, you allow them the dignity of their own emotional process. You are trusting them to be an adult, just as you are learning to be one.

Finding Your Calm

When emotions run high, we need a way to come back to ourselves. I like to think of these as "comforting balms" for the nervous system - little rituals that tell our bodies we are safe even when things feel tense. This is about re-parenting that part of you that still feels like a child in a principal's office when you've done nothing wrong. It's about creating a "safety net" that exists within your own skin.

For some, it's physical - tensing and releasing your muscles until the tightness leaves your jaw and your shoulders drop away from your ears. You might feel the tension in your hands, your calves, or your stomach. For others, it's a mental escape to a place that feels safe and untouchable, like a quiet stretch of beach you remember from childhood, the cool air of a mountain trail, or the corner of a favorite garden you visited years ago. Let the colors and sounds of that place wash over you until your pulse slows down.

You might also try a simple grounding exercise: notice three things you can see, two things you can hear, and one thing you can feel. The texture of your sleeve, the hum of the refrigerator, the light hitting the wall. These small, sensory observations pull you out of the emotional "swirl" and put you back into your body. They remind you that the room you are in is solid, the floor is beneath you, and you are safe within your own skin. This is the practice of becoming unshakeable - not because you don't feel things, but because you know how to return to your center.

Once the conversation is over, take a moment to look back. Not to criticize yourself or replay what you "should" have said - which is just another form of self-punishment - but with a sense of gentle curiosity. *What felt hardest? Where did the relief come in?* Maybe you noticed that the person's anger lasted only a minute before they moved on to another topic. Maybe you noticed that the world didn't actually fall apart when you weren't there to save the day. This isn't about being perfect. It's about turning the lights on in a dark room so you can see where the furniture is. The more you look, the less frightening the shadows become. You start to see that most "disasters" are just uncomfortable conversations, and you are more than capable of handling discomfort.

Saying Yes to You

We spend so much of our lives nodding along to things we don't actually want to do, driven by a fear of missing out, a fear of being "difficult," or a fear of letting someone down. We think we are being generous, but we are often just being fearful. We are spending our lives' currency on things that don't even matter to us, while the things that do matter - our health, our creativity, our rest - get pushed to the side.

But every time you say "no" to an obligation that drains you, you are saying "yes" to something else. You are saying "yes" to your own energy, your own values, and your own peace. You are saying "yes" to the version of you that isn't constantly running on empty. You are deciding that your life is more than a series of errands run for other people. You are choosing to be the protagonist of your own story rather than a supporting character in everyone else's. This "yes" is the foundation of a life that actually belongs to you.

It's an act of deep self-respect. It's a way of drawing a circle around your heart and saying, *"This space matters. My peace is not for sale."* It is the realization that your time is a finite, precious resource, and you are the only one who can decide how to spend it.

Think of Sarah, who stopped saying "yes" to every volunteer request and found her way back to her painting. At first, she felt like she was failing her community. She felt a phantom guilt whenever she sat at her easel, looking at the clock and wondering who was disappointed in her. But as the weeks went by, she realized she was a better mother and a more present friend because she wasn't constantly simmering with resentment. Her "yes" to herself made her other "yeses" meaningful again. She wasn't giving from an empty cup anymore; she was giving from the overflow. Her art became a source of life that spilled out into everything else she did.

Or James, who realized he didn't have to attend every social gathering just to prove he was a good friend. He found that the friends who truly mattered were still there, even when he chose a quiet night at home over a loud party. He learned that belonging doesn't require constant, exhausting presence; it requires honesty and shared truth. He discovered that the people who loved him wanted him rested and whole, not just present and depleted. He realized that a friendship that requires you to burn yourself out is not a friendship at all.

It wasn't weakness that kept them saying yes for so long. It was survival. It was the way they had learned to belong in a world that demands a lot. But choosing differently - choosing themselves - is how they finally started to live again. It wasn't about being selfish; it was about being sustainable. You cannot be a light for others if you have burned yourself down to the wick. Living an authentic life means admitting that you cannot do it all - and that you don't want to.

The People Who Hold You

None of us are meant to do this alone. We aren't built to be islands of perfect self-sufficiency, no matter how much our culture tells us we should be. In fact, trying to set boundaries in a vacuum is one of the hardest ways to do it. We need witnesses to our growth. We need people who see us struggling to say no and say, "I see you, and you're doing great."

Think of your life as a tapestry. The people who truly support you are the threads that hold it all together. They are the ones who remind you of your strength when you've forgotten it. They are the ones who say, *"I'm proud of you for saying no,"* instead of, *"But I really needed you to do this."* They are the safe harbors where you can drop your guard and be exactly as tired or as frustrated as you are. These people don't want the "polished" version of you; they want the real you.

Building this network takes a bit of intention and a lot of patience. It's the monthly coffee date where you don't have to perform. It's the quick phone call to "check in" just to hear a friendly voice. It's being brave enough to be vulnerable - to say to a friend, *"I'm trying to set better boundaries, and it feels really scary today. I feel like I'm doing it wrong."* When you share your struggles, you often find that the person across from you is struggling with the exact same thing. You give them permission to be human, too. You realize that your "struggle" is actually a shared experience of being alive.

You might experience what some call a "vulnerability hangover" - that feeling of exposure and regret after you've been honest about your needs. It's a heavy feeling, a mix of "why did I say that?" and the urge to hide. But it's a sign of growth. It's the feeling of new skin forming over an old wound. You aren't a burden for needing support. You are simply human, navigating a human life. We all need someone to remind us that we aren't "bad" for having needs, and that our worth isn't tied to how much we can do for others. A true support system isn't a group of people you have to please; it's a group of people who please you by being themselves.

A Gentle Hug for Yourself

Finally, remember to be kind to yourself after the "no" is spoken. This is perhaps the most important part of the inner work. The conversation with others is only half the battle; the conversation you have with yourself in the kitchen afterward is where the real change happens. This is where you decide whether you are going to be your own bully or your own best friend.

It's so easy to let guilt creep in. It's a habit we've spent decades perfecting, like a well-worn path through the woods. It's the old voice that tells you that you are selfish, cold, or lazy. When that old guilt arrives, try to treat yourself with the same warmth you'd give a dear friend.

If she told you she was exhausted and needed a break, you wouldn't tell her she was being selfish. You would tell her to rest. You would tell her she's earned it. You would probably offer to make her a cup of tea. Can you offer yourself the same tea?

You are allowed to prioritize your needs. You are allowed to have limits that don't require an explanation. You are allowed to be happy without an excuse. You are allowed to take up space in your own life.

It doesn't happen all at once. Be patient with the part of you that is still afraid.

Self-compassion isn't a luxury; it's the anchor that keeps you steady when the waves of other people's expectations start to crash in. It's the quiet voice that says, *"You did the best you could today, and that is enough."* It's the recognition that you are a work in progress, and that is a beautiful, sacred thing to be. It takes time to unlearn a lifetime of saying yes. Be patient with the part of you that is still afraid of being "too much" or "not enough."

As you move into your week, remember that boundaries aren't walls built to keep people out. They aren't meant to isolate you or make you untouchable. They are bridges that allow the right people in - the ones who respect your "no" as much as your "yes" - on terms that keep your heart whole. They allow connections based on truth and mutual respect rather than obligation and fear. They make room for a version of love that doesn't require you to disappear.

It doesn't happen all at once. It's one breath, one "no," and one moment of kindness at a time. It's a slow, steady turning toward yourself. And in that turning, you will find the peace you've been looking for all along. You were never lost; you were just waiting for yourself to come home. You are worth the effort it takes to get there.

Breadcrumbs

******** REVIEW********

YOU'RE PART OF THE Story Now

You've made it this far – proof that curiosity and courage are alive and well.
Whether you've been nodding along, laughing out loud, or quietly soaking it all in, you've already done something worth celebrating: you showed up for yourself.

If these pages have sparked a new idea, offered comfort, or simply given you a smile, would you consider sharing that experience?
Your review might be the little nudge someone else needs to pick up this book and begin their own journey.

Think of it as leaving a friendly breadcrumb trail – your words help future readers feel welcome and encouraged.

A few sentences is all it takes to:

Guide someone who's wondering if this book is for them

Help others discover a story or insight that could brighten their day

Support the work that brings books like this to life

Thank you for reading and for being part of this community of readers.

Your voice matters – please leave an honest review on the site where you found this book.

With gratitude and a happy little chair-dance of thanks,
Natalie

The Quiet Work of Building New Habits

Finding Your Center

Imagine you're at a neighborhood gathering. The air is familiar, the faces are friendly, and then it happens - someone asks for a favor that you don't have the room to give. It lands in your lap like an uninvited guest.

In the past, you might have felt that immediate heat in your chest, that pressure to be "helpful" or "the one who says yes." You probably said yes before you even realized your own heart was saying no. It was a habit, a silent contract you signed years ago to be the person who holds everything together. Many of us have spent decades wearing that mask of the "competent woman." We've become experts at anticipating what everyone else needs - the extra shifts at work, the bake sales, the emotional labor of smoothing over family tensions - often at the expense of our own quiet.

We were often raised to believe that our value was tied directly to our utility. We were the daughters of women who were the daughters of women who never said no, and so "helpful" became our primary identity. It was a survival strategy passed down through generations. We worry that if we stop being the "useful" one, we might stop being the "valued" one. There's a fear that if we aren't constantly solving problems, we'll become invisible to the people we love. But this constant output creates a kind of spiritual exhaustion. It's a low-grade hum of fatigue that we've mistaken for a normal way of living. We carry it in our tight jaws and our shallow breathing, a permanent state of readiness that never allows us to actually land in our own lives. We have become the infrastructure of everyone else's world while our own is crumbling for lack of maintenance.

But something is shifting now. You're beginning to see that a boundary isn't a wall you build to keep people out; it's more like a fence around a garden you're finally starting to tend. Inside that fence, you are growing things that matter: rest, creativity, and a little bit of peace. It's a way of saying, *This space is needed for me to stay whole.*

When we start to view our energy as a finite, precious resource rather than an endless well, the way we stand in that neighborhood gathering changes. You aren't being cold. You are simply being honest about what you have to give.

You realize that a "yes" born out of resentment isn't a gift to the other person anyway; it's a debt you're forcing yourself to pay, with interest that usually comes out of your sleep, your health, or your temper later that night. Setting a boundary is actually an act of kindness toward the relationship - it prevents the slow-poisoning effect of bitterness. It allows you to show up as your true self, rather than a hollowed-out version of who you think you should be. It says, "I value our connection enough to be honest with you."

Taking Small, Clear Steps

When we decide to change, we often want to fix everything by Tuesday. We want the "new version" of ourselves to arrive fully formed. Still, midlife has taught us that the most lasting shifts usually happen in the margins. It's the slow work of water carving through stone.

If we try to overhaul our entire lives in a single weekend, we usually just end up exhausted and back where we started, convinced that change is impossible. We set ourselves up for failure by trying to be "perfect" boundary-setters. Instead of setting massive, sweeping goals that feel like a burden, try looking for the small, doable things - the "energy leaks" that happen throughout your day. We spend so much of our lives responding to others' demands that we forget what our own pace feels like. We've been running at someone else's speed for so long that "slow" feels like "wrong" or "lazy."

Think of the small leaks. The person who always calls when they know you're sitting down to dinner, assuming you'll pick up because you always do. The group chat that pings incessantly with things that aren't your responsibility, but you feel the need to "fix" or moderate. The neighbor who assumes you'll take their package because you "work from home," even though you are actually in the middle of a workday. These are the places where we start.

Maybe it's deciding to wait ten minutes before replying to an "urgent" text that isn't actually an emergency. That ten-minute window is a sanctuary. It gives your nervous system a chance to settle and reminds you that you are the owner of your attention. You are not a 24-hour service station or a convenience store that never closes. Maybe it's choosing one evening a week where the phone stays in another room, or deciding that you won't check your emails after 7:00 PM.

These aren't just rules; they are tiny declarations of autonomy. They are ways of telling the world - and yourself - that you are not always "on call." Consider the "quick phone call" that you know will take an hour, or the "favor" that requires you to drive across town when you're already exhausted. Start noticing the physical pull toward compliance - that automatic lean forward, that slight tightening in the throat - and practice the quiet lean back.

We need our goals to be honest and reachable. If a goal feels like an exhausting chore, it probably isn't the right one for right now. Think about the areas of your life where you feel the most "leaking" of your energy. Is it a committee that has forgotten you have a life outside of their meetings? Start there. You don't have to quit the committee tomorrow; you might just decide to be the person who leaves at 8:00 PM, even if the meeting isn't finished. You might find that the world keeps spinning, even when you aren't the one holding it up.

Ask yourself: *Does this give me more room to breathe, or does it just add to the noise?* If it adds to the noise, let it go. There is no prize for the most difficult boundary. There is only the quiet reward of feeling like you own your time again.

A Place for Your Thoughts

There is something powerful about putting pen to paper. Not for a "perfect" record, or a list of things you did wrong, but just to get the weight of the day out of your head. In midlife, our minds are often crowded with the needs of aging parents, growing children, and the demands of our work. It is easy to lose the sound of our own voice in that chorus. We become a walking list of other people's requirements.

A boundaries journal doesn't need to be fancy. It doesn't need to be leather-bound or filled with profound insights. Sometimes the blank page itself feels like a demand, so keep it simple. It's just a place to notice things. It's a mirror that doesn't judge. You might write down a time you spoke up and felt a little rush of relief - a lightness in your shoulders you hadn't felt in years.

Or you might record a time you stayed silent and felt that familiar tightness in your chest, that "swallowed" feeling.

The body usually knows the truth before the mind does. When we ignore our boundaries, the body speaks in headaches, tight jaws, and shallow breaths. Journaling helps us bridge that gap. It allows us to look at a situation from the day and say, "I felt angry there. I wonder if a boundary was crossed."

Anger is often just a guardian at the gate, telling us that something we value - our time, our dignity, our peace - is being stepped on. It isn't a "bad" emotion; it's a diagnostic tool. In the past, you might have judged yourself for being "irritable," but now you can see that irritability was just your soul's way of saying it was out of room. When you start to listen to it, the anger often softens into clarity. It stops being a fire and starts being a signal.

Try asking yourself:

· What did I say "no" to today? How did my body feel in the moment afterward?

· Where did I feel pushed or invisible?

· What am I learning about what I actually need to feel rested?

This isn't about grading your performance or "mastering" a skill. It's about becoming a witness to your own life. When you see your boundaries written down, they become real. They move from a vague feeling in your gut to a tangible path forward. You begin to see patterns - the people who always push, the situations that always drain you, and the moments where you finally stood your ground.

Over time, these notes become a map of your own growth. They show you that you are changing, even on the days when you feel stuck. They provide evidence for the days when you feel like you haven't made any progress at all. You can look back and see: *A month ago, I couldn't have said that. Today, I did.* It's the difference between feeling like you're treading water and realizing you're actually swimming toward a shore.

Noticing the Ground You've Covered

We are often so focused on how far we have to go that we forget to look back at how far we've come. In the beginning, every "no" feels like a mountain. You might even feel a little bit of "boundary guilt" - that nagging voice that tells you you're being selfish or that you're letting people down. It's the voice of every person who ever benefited from you having no limits. It's the ghost of the "helper" you used to be.

But eventually, you'll look back and realize you've been walking on level ground for a while. The guilt fades, replaced by a sense of calm. You start to realize that by saying no to the things that drain you, you have more "yes" for the things you truly love. You aren't just protecting yourself; you're preserving your capacity to be present for the people who actually matter. You're learning that a boundary isn't a rejection of others; it's an invitation to a more honest connection.

Tracking your progress isn't about checking boxes on a list. It's about noticing the shifts in your internal weather. It's noticeable that the "uninvited guest" request at the party didn't make you panic this time. It's realizing you haven't felt that specific kind of Sunday-night resentment in a few weeks because you've protected your weekend. It's the moment you realize you didn't spend three hours agonizing over an email reply - you just sent it and moved on.

You may even notice how others react. Sometimes, people who are used to your lack of boundaries will push back. They might call you "difficult" or "different." They might try to guilt-trip you into your old roles. In those moments, remind yourself that you aren't becoming a villain; you are simply becoming a person with edges.

Celebrate these moments not necessarily with a grand gesture, but with a quiet acknowledgment. Perhaps it's just a long exhale or a moment of stillness over your morning coffee. Acknowledge that you are honoring yourself. It wasn't weakness that kept you quiet before; it was survival. You did what you had to do to keep things moving. You were the glue for so many people. But now, you're choosing something else. You're choosing to thrive.

When we celebrate the small wins, we are telling our brain that this new way of living is safe. We are teaching ourselves that the world doesn't end when we say "no." In fact, for many of us, the world finally begins. You become more authentic, and ironically, the people who truly love you usually appreciate that honesty. They would rather have the real you than the tired, resentful version you were offering before. They start to see you as a person, not just a service provider.

The Grace of Starting Over

Life is messy. A strategy that worked last month might feel impossible today. Maybe work gets busy, or a family member needs extra care, and your boundaries feel like they're slipping through your fingers. You might find yourself back in that old habit of over-explaining or over-committing, trying to be everything to everyone once again.

It's easy to feel like you've failed when this happens. You might think, *I thought I was past this.* But boundaries are meant to be living things. They are not concrete walls; they are more like the banks of a river. They need to breathe and stretch as the volume of their lives changes. Sometimes the river is high, and the banks need to be sturdy to prevent flooding. This might happen during a family crisis, a health scare, or a major work transition. In those seasons, your boundaries might look like doing the bare minimum for others so you can focus on the crisis at hand. Sometimes the river is low, and things can be more fluid.

If a boundary isn't working, you don't abandon the effort - you just adjust the line.

Maybe you realized that saying "no" to every Saturday commitment was too rigid, leaving you feeling isolated. So, you move the line to "no Saturdays before noon." That isn't failure; it's wisdom. It's the result of listening to your life. It takes a lot of heart to be flexible without giving yourself away. It requires us to constantly check in and ask: *Is this still serving me? Is this still true?*

Forgive yourself for the days you get it wrong. The goal isn't perfection; it's presence. Every time you realize you've let a boundary slip, you've actually made progress, because you *noticed* it. That awareness is the first step back to your center. The faster you can forgive yourself, the faster you can get back to tending your garden. The "reset" is always available to you, in every new breath. You don't have to wait until Monday to start again. You can start again right now.

The Wisdom of Patience

We live in a world that demands instant results, but the soul moves at a different pace. We want the relief of a balanced life right now, but growth is rarely a straight line. It's more like a spiral - we often circle back to the same challenges, but each time we face them, we do so with a little more strength and a little more perspective. You might find yourself dealing with the same "pushy" relative for the tenth time, but notice that this time, your heart didn't race quite as fast. You didn't feel the need to justify your choices. That is what progress looks like.

Think of it like a garden in winter. To the naked eye, nothing is happening. The ground is hard, the trees are bare, and everything looks dormant. It can feel discouraging, like all your hard work has come to a standstill. But underneath the cold soil, roots are deepening. They are gathering strength, storing energy, and preparing for what's next. They are doing the quiet, invisible work that makes the spring possible. Without that winter rest, there would be no flowers.

Your growth is like that. Some days, it will feel like you aren't making any progress at all. You'll slip back into old patterns. You'll say "yes" when you meant "no," and you'll feel that old familiar sting of regret. You might feel like you're right back at the beginning.

When that happens, be gentle. Patience isn't just about waiting for things to change; it's about how you treat yourself while the change is happening. It's about refusing to be your own harshest critic. Change is a slow, gradual unfolding. It's a series of small, mundane choices that eventually add up to a different kind of life. It's the choice to take a nap instead of doing one more load of laundry. It's the choice to let someone else be the "hero" for once. It is the choice to say "not today" so that you can say "yes" to your own well-being.

Trust the process. Trust that every time you honor your own limits, even the small ones, you are reclaiming a piece of yourself. You are teaching the people around you how to treat you, but more importantly, you are teaching yourself that you are worth the effort. You are learning that your value isn't tied to how much you can do for others, but in who you are when you are simply at rest.

You're not just setting boundaries. You're building a life that actually fits who you are today, not who you were twenty years ago. You are creating space for your own joy, your own rest, and your own voice. It doesn't happen overnight. It happens one quiet step at a time, until one day you wake up and realize you finally feel at home in your own life. You realize the fence is strong, the garden is blooming, and you finally have enough room to breathe. You've reclaimed your center, and that is where everything begins.

The Silent Weight of Fear

You know the feeling. It's that sudden, sharp tightening in your chest when you realize you need to say no, but the word feels stuck in your throat. It's the knot in your stomach that tells you a conflict is coming, even if it's a small one. It's that heavy heat that rises in your neck when you think about disappointing someone.

We've all been there.

Fear isn't just an emotion we study in books or talk about in therapy; it's a physical presence. It sits in the room with us like an uninvited guest. It's there when we're deciding whether to tell a friend we can't make it to her dinner party because we're simply too exhausted to perform. It's there when we're about to tell a colleague that we can't take on another project, even though we know they're struggling, too. It whispers that we are being difficult. It warns us that if we speak up, we might lose the very thing we're trying to protect: our connection to others.

In this season of life - this midlife reset - fear often acts as a gatekeeper. It stands between the woman you are - the tired one, the one who needs a break, the one who finally wants to be honest - and the woman you think you're supposed to be. It tells you that saying no is a risk you can't afford to take. It tells you that your worth is tied to your availability. And so, we wait. We retreat. We let the moment pass, and the boundary remains unbuilt. We choose the comfort of others over our own integrity.

Confrontation is perhaps the heaviest fear many of us carry. We imagine the worst. We see the raised voices, the rolling eyes, or the cold, heavy silence that follows a disagreement. We play out the scene in our minds, and we decide that our own comfort isn't worth the price of that discord. It feels safer to stay quiet. It feels easier to just do the thing we don't want to do than to handle the energy of someone else's disappointment.

But silence has a cost, too. It's a debt we pay with our own vitality.

The Stories We Tell in the Dark

These fears don't come from nowhere. They aren't a sign that you are failing or weak. They are the result of years of quiet lessons, societal whispers, and the way we've learned to survive in a world that often rewards us for being "easy" and "agreeable." For decades, many of us have been praised for our selflessness, which is often just a polite way of saying we have no boundaries.

There is a cycle to this. When we avoid a difficult conversation, we feel a sudden rush of relief. The knot in our stomach loosens. The pressure in our chest evaporates. We think *I dodged it.* We feel like we've won a small victory because we avoided the friction.

But that relief is a bit of a trick. It's a "false friend." It feels like a reward, but it's actually a brick in a wall we're building around ourselves. Each time we pull back to stay safe, the wall gets a little higher, and the world outside - the world where we are honest and firm - gets a little harder to reach. We become prisoners of our own avoidance. The relief lasts for an hour, but the resentment lasts for weeks.

We also have a habit of telling ourselves stories about the future. We call it "catastrophizing" in psychology, but in real life, it's just the "what-ifs."

What if she never speaks to me again? What if they think I'm selfish? What if I'm not as necessary as I thought I was?

We take a small refusal - like saying "I can't host the holiday this year" - and we turn it into a total abandonment. We convince ourselves that our friends will stop calling or our family will stop loving us. We see the worst-case scenario as the only scenario. And when we look at it that way, setting a boundary doesn't just feel hard - it feels like an act of self-destruction.

It doesn't happen all at once. The shift happens in the small moments, in the quiet choices we make every day.

Finding Your Way Back to "No"

Breaking these patterns isn't about becoming fearless. It's about learning to walk alongside the fear. It's about noticing the fear, acknowledging its presence, and then choosing to move anyway.

You don't have to start by tackling your biggest, most terrifying boundary. You don't start by calling your mother-in-law and telling her she can't stay for two weeks. You start small. You start with the low-stakes "no."

Think about the cashier who asks if you want to donate two dollars to a charity you've never heard of. Or the neighbor who catches you at the mailbox and starts a conversation you don't have time for. Maybe it's a phone call from a telemarketer or an invitation to a "quick" Zoom meeting that you know will last an hour.

Practice the "no" there. You let yourself feel that tiny spike of discomfort - that little "oh no, I'm being rude" feeling - and then you watch it fade. You realize that the world didn't end. The cashier didn't chase you to the car. The neighbor didn't stop liking you; they just moved on to someone else. You survived the "no."

It helps to see it before it happens. Close your eyes for a moment and imagine yourself saying it. Don't imagine a fight. Don't imagine you being defensive or angry. Imagine a calm, clear sentence. "I can't do that right now, but thank you for asking." Imagine the other person simply nodding and saying, "Okay."

We spend so much time rehearsing the disaster that we forget to rehearse the peace. We forget that most people are actually quite fine with boundaries when they are delivered with kindness and clarity.

An Invitation: Mapping the Fear

I want you to think about the boundaries you've been avoiding. Don't judge them - just look at them. Treat them like a map of a territory you're about to explore.

Try to list them out. Which ones feel like a "2" on a scale of discomfort? Which ones feel like a "10"?

Maybe the "2" means no to an extra task at the PTA meeting or to telling a friend you can't talk on the phone tonight. Maybe a "5" means you won't check emails after 7:00 PM. And maybe the "10" is telling your partner that you need one night a week entirely to yourself - no cooking, no kids, no questions.

Start with the "2." Practice it. Feel the weight of it in your hands. Notice how your body reacts when you say it. When you realize you can handle the "2," the "3" doesn't look quite so daunting. The "10" is still there, waiting for you, but you're building the muscles you need to carry it.

It wasn't weakness that kept you silent. It was survival. You were protecting your peace the only way you knew how. But you don't have to just survive anymore. You are allowed to live.

The Roots of the Quiet Self

Think back to a young girl you once knew. Maybe she's you.

She is watching the adults in her life. She is learning when to speak and when to be still. She is absorbing the messages conveyed by a raised eyebrow, a sharp tone, or a heavy sigh of disappointment. She learns that when she is quiet and helpful, the room stays calm. She learns that when she has no needs, she is "easy to love."

Our self-worth isn't something we're born with; it's something that was shaped for us, long before we had a say in it. If you grew up in a house where your value was tied to how much you helped, or how little you complained, it makes sense that you struggle with boundaries now. You were taught that being "good" meant being "available." You were taught that "selfish" was the worst thing a woman could be.

As we move into midlife, these old lessons start to feel tight. They're like a pair of shoes we've outgrown but are still trying to wear. We look around at the curated lives on our screens - the women who seem to have "perfect" boundaries and "perfect" lives - and we feel the sting of comparison. We see women who seem to have it all together, and we assume that because we feel exhausted and overwhelmed, we must be doing something wrong. We feel we haven't "earned" the right to put ourselves first because we haven't reached that invisible standard of "enough."

But self-worth isn't a prize you win. It's the ground you stand on.

When you don't believe you are worthy of your own time, asserting yourself feels like a performance you haven't rehearsed. You worry that if you say no, people will finally see the "selfish" or "lazy" person you're secretly afraid you are. You worry that the mask will slip.

It's hard to stand up for someone you don't quite believe in yet. It's hard to protect a space that you don't think you deserve to occupy.

To change this, we have to change the way we talk to ourselves. Not with loud, aggressive "boss babe" talk or empty motivational quotes, but with quiet, honest truths. We have to start giving ourselves the permission we've been waiting for others to give us.

"I am a person with needs." "My energy is not an infinite resource." "I am allowed to be tired." "I don't have to explain my 'no'."

It feels awkward at first. It feels like wearing someone else's coat. It might even feel "wrong" or "mean." But if you keep saying it - if you keep acknowledging that your needs matter simply because you are a human being, not because of what you do for others - the coat starts to fit. The truth starts to settle into your bones.

A Moment for Reflection: The Self-Compassion Journal

Take a moment to look back. Think about a time you felt small, or a time you felt you weren't enough. Maybe it was a moment this morning, or maybe it was something that happened thirty years ago.

Instead of looking at it with shame, look at it with kindness. Write down how that younger version of you felt in that moment. What was your younger self afraid of? What did she think would happen if she spoke up?

And then, write down what you know now.

You might say: *I felt like I had to say yes to stay safe and loved. I understand why I did that. I was just a girl trying to find her way. But I am an adult now. I am safe, and I can choose differently. I can handle someone being a little bit annoyed with me.*

Building self-esteem isn't a project with a deadline. It isn't a "fix." It's a slow, steady return to yourself. It's learning to be your own best friend.

The Stories We Believe

We often live at the intersection of our thoughts and our actions, but we rarely stop to see how much they influence each other. Our thoughts are the architects of our reality.

The stories we tell ourselves are often like mirrors in a funhouse. They distort the truth. We fall into "all-or-nothing" thinking: *If I'm not the perfect mother, I'm a failure. If I can't do this job perfectly, I shouldn't be here.* This kind of thinking leaves no room for the messy, beautiful reality of being human. It makes every boundary feel like a high-stakes gamble.

Or we overgeneralize. We remember the one time a friend got upset when we set a boundary, and we decided that "it never works out" or "people can't handle the truth." We take one bad experience and turn it into a universal law.

Breaking these patterns is about becoming a witness to your own mind. It's about slowing down enough to see the thought before it becomes an action. When a thought like *They'll hate me if I say no* pops up, don't argue with it. Don't try to crush it. Just look at it.

Ask yourself: *Is that really true? Do I have proof for that, or is that just a story I've been telling for twenty years? If a friend said no to me, would I hate her?*

Usually, the answer is a quiet *no*.

It's about shifting the perspective, just an inch.

Instead of thinking, *"I can't say no because she'll be upset," try thinking, "She might be disappointed, and that's okay."*

I can handle her disappointment. I can't handle my own burnout.

It's a small shift. But it changes the entire landscape of the conversation.

Consider Sarah. She spent years staying late at the office, taking on everyone else's slack, because she was terrified of disappointing her boss. She thought her value was her availability. She thought if she wasn't the first one in and the last one out, she was replaceable.

Through a lot of quiet work, she started to see that her boss actually valued her *work*, not her exhaustion. She realized that by being constantly available, she was teaching people to undervalue her time. She started small - leaving at 5:00 PM once a week. She felt sick the first time she did it. She felt like everyone was watching her walk out the door.

But she survived. No one fired her. In fact, no one even mentioned it. Then she did it twice a week.

She realized that the fear was a ghost. It didn't have a body. It couldn't actually hurt her. The only thing that was hurting her was the weight of the cloak she was choosing to wear.

What about you? What ghosts are you letting run your life? What "rules" are you following that no one actually wrote down?

You don't have to be perfect at this. Boundary-setting isn't about the perfect response or the perfect tone of voice; it's about the honest one. It's about making progress, one small decision at a time. It's about choosing yourself, even when your hands are shaking.

The Imprint of Childhood

We are all carrying the children we used to be. We are all, in some way, responding to the environments that raised us.

Our parents were our first maps. We watched how they handled their own lives, their own needs, and their own conflicts. If your mother always put herself last - if she was the one who ate the burnt toast and never sat down until everyone else was finished - you learned that "love" looks like "sacrifice." You learned that to be a woman is to be a martyr.

If your father was distant or critical unless you were achieving something - if his love felt like a reward for a job well done - you learned that "worth" looks like "performance." You learned that you are only as good as your last accomplishment.

These early messages create a sort of emotional gravity. They pull us back toward compliance. They make us feel a strange sense of guilt when we try to do things differently, as if we're betraying our history or insulting our parents' choices.

But you can love your past and still decide not to live there. You can honor your parents' sacrifices without repeating their mistakes.

There is a way to heal these old wounds. It's called "inner child work," but really, it's just about being the parent to yourself that you needed back then. It's about looking at that younger version of you and saying, "I see you. I see how hard you're trying to be good. But you don't have to be perfect to be loved."

It’s about acknowledging that the little girl who was taught to be quiet was just doing her best to survive. And then, it’s about telling her - firmly and gently - that she’s allowed to speak up now. She’s allowed to have a voice. She’s allowed to say "no."

Try writing a letter to that younger version of yourself. Don't overthink it. Just write. Tell your younger self it’s okay to be difficult. Tell her she doesn't have to earn her place at the table. Tell her that her time and her peace are sacred. This isn't about erasing the past - it’s about integrating it. It’s about writing a new ending to a story that started a long time ago.

Letting Go of "Perfect"

Perfectionism is a heavy, suffocating cloak. It promises to keep us safe by making us irreproachable. It tells us that if we never make a mistake, no one can ever criticize us. But perfectionism is just a high-end form of fear.

If we think we have to set the "perfect" boundary with the "perfect" words at the "perfect" time, we will never do it. We will wait for a moment of absolute clarity and confidence that never comes. We will wait for the stars to align, while our energy continues to drain away.

We worry that if we make a mistake - if we're too harsh, or if we stumble over our words, or if we get emotional - we've failed. We think that if the other person gets angry, our boundary wasn't "good enough."

But the goal isn't to be a boundary-setting machine. The goal isn't to win every argument. The goal is to be a person who is learning to be honest.

"Good enough" is a beautiful, liberating phrase.

A "good enough" no, even if it's delivered with a shaky voice and a red face, is infinitely better than a "perfect" yes that you don't mean.

When you stop trying to be flawless, you give yourself room to breathe. You allow yourself to be human. You allow yourself to be a work in progress. And strangely, when you allow yourself to be human, other people often respond with a human kind of respect. They see the effort. They see the honesty. And they often step back to give you the space you're asking for.

Perfectionism says: *I must be beyond reproach.* Integrity says: *I must be true to myself.*

Choose integrity. It's much lighter to carry.

The Words We Choose to Believe

Every day, from the moment we open our eyes, we have a choice about the words we say to ourselves. We have a choice about which voices we listen to.

This isn't about empty slogans, "toxic positivity," or shouting at yourself in the mirror. It's about reinforcing the truth in the quiet moments.

When you wake up, before the world starts asking things of you - before the phone pings and the house wakes up - tell yourself something true. "I am worthy of care, regardless of what I get done today." "My time belongs to me first." "I can handle the discomfort of a 'no'."

These aren't magic spells. They won't make the fear disappear instantly. They won't stop the knot in your stomach from forming. But they give you a place to stand when the fear arrives. They give you a tether. They remind you of who you are when the world tries to tell you who you should be.

Emma, a woman I know, used to struggle with saying no to her family. She was the "fixer." If someone needed money, a ride, or a shoulder to cry on at 2:00 AM, they called Emma. She was exhausted, resentful, and losing her sense of self.

She started using a simple phrase: "My time is valuable." She didn't say it to them at first; she said it to herself. She whispered it while she was doing the dishes. She thought it while she was driving. After a few weeks, she found she didn't have to say it as much. She just *felt* it. It became part of her internal architecture.

And when her sister asked her for a major favor that Emma truly didn't have the energy for, the "no" came out naturally. "I'd love to help, but I just don't have the capacity for that right now."

Her sister was surprised. She was even a little annoyed. But Emma didn't collapse. She didn't apologize a thousand times. She stood her ground with her "no."

It wasn't a battle. It was just a fact.

You say yes. Even when something in you says no. It doesn't happen all at once. It's a slow turning of the tide. It wasn't weakness. It was survival.

By understanding the "why" behind your fear - by looking at the roots and the stories and the childhood imprints - you're already halfway to the "how." You are building a foundation of confidence that doesn't rely on being perfect or being liked by everyone. You are learning to trust yourself. You are learning that your "no" is just as holy as your "yes."

And that is where the real reset begins in the quiet, steady reclamation of your own life.

The Unspoken Language of Boundaries

THERE IS A SPECIFIC kind of silence that happens at a family dinner or a busy office gathering. You're sitting there, perhaps the smell of something home-cooked is in the air, or the hum of the printer is in the background, and someone leans in. A cousin, a colleague, a friend. They ask for a favor - something small on the surface, but something you know will cost you your last bit of energy for the week.

In that moment, there is a pause. It's heavy. You feel the weight of the expectation, and you feel the "yes" forming in your throat simply because it's the path of least resistance. You might even feel your head nodding before your brain has fully processed the request. It's a form of social mimicry we've perfected over the decades. You wonder how to say no without breaking the connection, without being the one who "dampens the mood."

We've been taught that being "good" means being available. We have been raised to believe that any friction we cause is a failure of character, a crack in our carefully maintained exterior. For many of us, our identity has been built on the foundation of being "the easy one" - the one who doesn't complain, the one who carries the extra load, the one who makes sure everyone else's glass is full. At the same time, ours sits empty on the counter. We've spent years smoothing things over, anticipating needs before they are even spoken, and making sure everyone else is comfortable. We have become experts at the "polite smile" that hides a growing hollow in our chest. We have learned to be the air in the room: invisible, essential, and easily taken for granted.

But that friction is often just the sound of two different lives trying to occupy the same space. It is the sound of you finally taking up room. It is the necessary noise of a person returning to themselves. It isn't a betrayal of others; it is a commitment to the truth of your own capacity. When we stop being the air, we start being the person. And people have edges.

This is where we begin to look at the language we use, not as a set of scripts to memorize, but as a way to bridge the gap between what we need and what the world expects from us. It is about learning to speak from the center of yourself, rather than from the edges where you are trying to please everyone else. It is a slow turning, a redirection of your attention from *their* comfort to *your* truth.

Finding the Words

We often think of communication as a performance, but it's actually more like a clear path through a garden. When the path is overgrown with vague "maybes" and "I'll try to's," everyone gets lost. We think we are being kind by being indirect, but ambiguity is often where resentment grows. It's like trying to drive through a thick fog without your lights on. You might move forward, but you're constantly bracing for a collision.

When we move toward clarity, we aren't being harsh. We are being kind. There is a profound mercy in letting someone know exactly where you stand. It saves them the work of guessing, and it saves you the work of pretending. Think of the energy you waste wondering if they understood your subtle hint, or the hours spent worrying if you've "led them on" by not being clear. When you are clear, that energy comes back to you. You can use it for your own life.

Using "I" statements isn't a psychological trick; it's a way of taking ownership of our own space. There is a quiet strength in saying, "I'm not available for that," or "I need to focus on my own work right now." It isn't an attack on the other person. It is a simple statement of fact. For many of us in this stage of life, we have spent decades using "we" or "they" to describe our needs, hiding behind the requirements of our children, our partners, or our jobs. We've said, "The kids need to get home," when what we meant was, "I am exhausted, and I need to go."

When we reclaim the "I," we reclaim our identity. We stop being representatives of our family or our company and start being ourselves. This transition is uncomfortable. It feels exposed. But it is also the only place where a true connection can happen. You cannot truly be "with" someone if the "I" is missing. You are just a shadow responding to a light.

You say yes. Even when something in you says no.

It takes practice to find the words that fit your mouth. You might start with something gentle: *"I prefer not to."* It's a soft limit, but it's still a limit. It allows you to move through your day with a sense of agency. Think of the requests that come in - the extra committee, the week-end project, the "quick" phone call that you know will take an hour. When a manager or a friend asks for more of you than you have to give, saying, *"I appreciate that you trust me with this, but I need to protect my evening,"* isn't a failure of work ethic or friendship. It's an act of sustainability.

If we don't protect our time, we eventually have nothing left to give to the things that actually matter. We become ghosts in our own lives, going through the motions but never fully present.

It wasn't weakness that made you say yes before. It was survival. It was the way you learned to stay safe and loved in a world that rewards compliance. But now, we are looking for something more than just getting by. We are looking for a way to live that doesn't require us to disappear.

The Internal Rehearsal

Before we ever speak a boundary, we usually have a conversation with ourselves. We call this the "Internal Rehearsal." You spend the car ride to the office or the hours before a family gathering running through every possible scenario. *If they say this, I'll say that. If they look disappointed, I'll offer a compromise.* We do this because we are afraid of the reaction. We are afraid of the silence that follows a "no."

But the rehearsal is often more exhausting than the conversation itself. It is a form of emotional labor that we perform in the dark, spinning wheels that never touch the ground. We are trying to control the other person's emotions before they even feel them.

Part of the midlife reset is learning to stop the rehearsal. It is trusting that you don't need a script to be worthy of your own time. You don't need to be prepared for every possible rebuttal. You just need to be prepared to be honest. When you stop rehearsing, you start breathing. You move from a state of defense to a state of presence. You realize you are responsible for your "no," but not for their reaction to it.

The Polite Trap and the "Just" Habit

We often fall into the trap of over-explaining. When we say "no," we feel the need to justify our existence with a list of excuses. We list our appointments, our headaches, our busy schedules, hoping the other person will grant us "permission" to have a boundary. We wait for them to say, "Oh, I see, you really *are* busy, so it's okay."

But every excuse we give is an invitation for the other person to negotiate. If you say, "I can't help because I have a doctor's appointment," they might say, "Oh, I can wait until you're done." Suddenly, your boundary has become a debate. You find yourself trapped in a logic puzzle where you have to prove you're "busy enough" to earn your own time. This over-explanation is an apology for having a life that belongs to you. It is a way of saying, *"I'm sorry, I'm not who you need me to be right now."*

The quietest truth is often the strongest: *"I can't do that right now."* You don't need a reason to be tired. You don't need a reason to need space. Your "no" is a complete sentence. It stands on its own, requiring no scaffolding of excuses to support it.

Watch, too, for the "just" habit. "I'm *just* checking in," or "I *just* wondered if..." This little word is a way of shrinking ourselves. It's a way of saying, *I know I'm taking up space, and I'm sorry about it.* It minimizes our requests and our presence before we've even finished the sentence. When you catch yourself adding a "just," try removing it. See how it feels to speak without apologizing for the sound of your own voice. It wasn't an interruption. It was a contribution. It wasn't a bother. It was a bridge.

The Power of What Isn't Said

Sometimes, the most important part of a boundary isn't the "no" itself, but the consequence we are willing to name. This doesn't have to be a threat; in fact, it shouldn't be. It's just a map. It's letting someone know where the cliff edge is before they fall over it. If a colleague constantly interrupts your flow, you might say, *"I need this hour to be quiet; otherwise, I won't be able to finish this report on time."* You are simply showing them the landscape. You are telling them how the world works for you.

When we omit the "why" or the consequence, we leave people guessing. We expect them to read our minds, and when they don't, we feel betrayed. We carry the weight of their ignorance as if it were a personal slight. This is how the "silent treatment" or passive-aggression starts. We haven't given them the map, yet we're angry they're lost.

By naming the result of an action - "If we keep talking now, I'm going to be late for my daughter's game" - we are offering the other person a chance to be a partner in our boundaries rather than an intruder. It is an invitation to respect. When we see it this way, the "script" disappears. We aren't managing people; we are narrating our needs. It becomes less about control and more about honesty. You are giving them the information they need to be a better friend, partner, or colleague to you.

The Art of Being Present and the "WAIT" Principle

We've all been in those conversations where words are being exchanged, but no one is actually there. You're nodding, they're talking, but you're both just waiting for your turn to speak. Or worse, you're already formulating your defense while they are still explaining their feelings. You are miles away, caught in the tangle of your own thoughts, preparing for a battle that hasn't even begun.

Active listening is often taught as a technique - nodding three times, mirroring phrases - but in our midlife reset, we see it as a form of presence. It's about the space between the words. It's the willingness to sit in the silence after someone finishes speaking, rather than rushing to fill it. When we truly listen, we aren't just hearing a request; we are hearing the person behind it. We are hearing their fear, their excitement, or their own struggle with boundaries.

There is a simple acronym that can help in these moments: **WAIT**. *Why Am I Talking?* Sometimes we talk to fix things, to avoid discomfort, or to fill a gap that feels too vulnerable. We offer advice when someone just needs to be heard. We say "yes" when we want to say "no" because silence feels like a judgment. But when we ask ourselves *why* we are speaking, we often find that the most powerful response is silence.

When you say, *"So, if I'm hearing you correctly, you're feeling overwhelmed by this project,"* you aren't just repeating what they said. You are offering them a mirror. You are saying, *I see you.* And funny enough, when someone feels seen, their need to push against your boundaries often softens. They don't have to shout if they know you can hear them.

It doesn't happen all at once. It's a slow unfolding of trust.

There is a specific kind of power in silence during a negotiation. When you state your boundary - "I can't take on that extra shift" - and then you *stop talking*, you allow the boundary to settle. We often try to fill that silence with apologies or justifications, which weakens the boundary. Let the silence do the work for you. It is the foundation upon which your "no" stands. It shows that you are comfortable with your decision, even if the other person isn't.

The Body's Honest Testimony

Our bodies often speak long before our mouths do. You might be saying, "I'm happy to help," but your shoulders are up near your ears, and your arms are tightly crossed. Your stomach might feel like it's in a knot, or your breath might become shallow and quick. Maybe you feel a sudden heat in your neck or a buzzing in your ears. We send mixed signals when our words and our bodies aren't on the same team. People can sense that friction; they feel the "no" in your energy even if they hear the "yes" in your voice. This creates a subtle sense of mistrust and unease in the relationship.

Your body is a compass. It tells you when a boundary is being crossed before your brain even has a word for it. It might be a sudden tension in your jaw when the phone rings and you see a certain name on the screen. Or a feeling of heaviness in your chest when someone asks for "just five minutes" at the end of a long day. These aren't inconveniences; they are information. They are your internal system telling you that your reservoir is low.

Standing tall, keeping your breath steady, and looking someone in the eye - these aren't just "power poses." There are ways of grounding ourselves in our own truth. When you assert a boundary, let your body support you. A calm voice carries more weight than a loud one. It's the difference between a lighthouse and a flare; one is a steady guide, the other is a cry for help.

The next time you feel a request coming in that you want to decline, pause. Feel your feet on the floor. Wiggle your toes. Take a breath into your belly. Let your body settle before you let your voice speak. When you speak from a grounded place, your "no" has a different frequency. It sounds less like an apology and more like a boundary. It feels solid, both to you and to the person hearing it.

Negotiation as an Act of Empathy

In a world that often feels like a series of battles, empathy can feel like a risk. We worry that if we understand the other person too much, we'll lose our ground. We think that empathy means agreement, but it doesn't. You can deeply understand why someone wants something from you and still say no to them. You can hold their disappointment and your boundary in the same hand.

But empathetic negotiation isn't about giving in. It's about seeing the whole room. It's about recognizing that the person across from you has their own set of pressures, fears, and unspoken needs. They are likely struggling with their own boundaries, too.

Think of a mother negotiating boundaries with her adult child. The child wants more of her time, and the mother needs more of her own space. Without empathy, it's a fight about "selfishness." With empathy, the mother can say, *"I know you're going through a lot right now, and you value our time together, and I value it too. I also need my Saturday mornings to recharge so I can be fully present with you when we are together."* If you're asking for flexible hours, and you know your manager is worried about the team's output, acknowledge that. *"I know the team's goals are the priority, and I share that concern. I believe working from home on Tuesdays will actually help me meet those goals more effectively because I can do the deep work without interruptions."* You aren't fighting them. You are solving a problem together. You move from being adversaries to being allies in the same story. This doesn't mean you'll always get exactly what you want. Still, it means the conversation stays respectful, and the relationship remains intact.

Assertiveness, Aggression, and the Third Way

There is a difference between being assertive and being aggressive. We often confuse the two, especially if we were raised to believe that any form of self-advocacy is "rude" or "unfeminine." We were taught to be the "Good Woman" - the one who is always pleasant, always accommodating, and never the source of conflict.

Aggression is a wildfire - it's hot, it's destructive, and it leaves a lot of ash behind. It seeks to dominate and win. It comes from a place of fear and insecurity, the belief that if you don't fight, you'll be erased. Assertiveness is more like a steady flame in a hearth. It provides warmth and light, but it stays within its bounds. It seeks to be understood and respected. It comes from a place of worthiness.

Aggression says, *"You always ignore my emails, and it's incredibly disrespectful."* Assertiveness says, *"I feel frustrated when my questions aren't answered, because it stalls my progress on the project. How can we make sure we're communicating more effectively?"*

But there is a third way we often fall into: Passive-Aggression. This is the shadow of the Good Woman. It's the heavy sigh when we agree to something we don't want to do. It's the "fine" that clearly means things are not fine. It's the subtle barb disguised as a joke. Passive-aggression is just a boundary that was never spoken out loud. It is the pipe leak that eventually floods the room. Choosing assertiveness is a way to stop the leaks. It is a way to be honest before the pressure becomes too much to bear.

The Vulnerability Hangover

A phenomenon often occurs after we set a boundary for the first time. We call it the vulnerability hangover. You say "no," you stand your ground, and then an hour later, you are flooded with guilt. You replay the conversation a thousand times in your head. You wonder if they're mad at you. You wonder if you were too harsh. You might even feel a physical "come down" - a shakiness or a sudden exhaustion.

It feels like a mistake. You feel like you've broken something precious.

But it isn't a mistake. That guilt is just the sound of old habits trying to pull you back into the "Good Woman" role. It is the discomfort of growth. You are breaking a pattern that has been in place for decades, and your system is sounding an alarm because it feels unfamiliar. It feels "unsafe" to the part of you that learned to survive by being small.

When the hangover hits, don't rush to apologize. Don't take the "no" back. Just sit with the discomfort. Remind yourself: *"It wasn't a failure. It was a beginning."* Breathe through the guilt. It will pass, and on the other side of it, you will find a version of yourself that is a little more solid, a little more real. You are building muscle. Muscle always aches before it grows strong.

Creating the Space

Finally, we have to look at the environments we live and work in. Some spaces make it very hard to have boundaries. If you work in a culture where "last one to leave wins," or live in a home where your labor is invisible and expected, speaking up will feel like an uphill climb. It can feel like you're trying to plant a garden in a desert.

But we can begin to build "boundary-friendly" cultures in small ways. It starts with modeling. When you respect your own boundaries, you give others permission to do the same. You become a permission slip for everyone else in the room. You show them that it is possible to be both kind and firm. You show them that saying "no" doesn't mean the world ends.

In your home, it might be a weekly check-in where everyone gets to say what they need for the upcoming days. *"I need two hours on Saturday morning to just be by myself. How can we make that work for everyone?"* It might mean letting the dishes sit in the sink for an hour so you can sit on the porch and breathe. It might mean saying, "I'm not available for phone calls after 8 PM."

In your office, it might be a team norm that says "no emails after 6 PM" or "no meetings on Friday afternoons." These aren't just rules; they are ways of saying that we value the humans behind the work. There are ways of acknowledging that we are more than our productivity. We are people with lives, families, and a need for rest. When you honor your own limits, you teach people how to treat you. And more importantly, you teach them how to treat themselves.

The Invisible Labor of Midlife: The Hinge

In midlife, we are often the "hinge" of the family. We are the ones holding the door open for everyone else. We are looking after aging parents whose needs are increasing and whose worlds are shrinking. We are looking after children - whether they are young and demanding or transitioning into adulthood and still needing a safe place to land. We are also often at the peak of our professional responsibilities, managing teams or projects that require our constant attention.

This is the season where boundaries are most difficult, and most necessary. We are the "default" person for everyone. If a parent falls, we get the call. If a child is sick, we are the ones who adjust. We are the "emotional architect" of our lives, the one who knows where everyone is, what they need, and how they feel. This is heavy labor, largely invisible.

There is a specific kind of grief in setting boundaries with aging parents. You are watching them lose their independence, and you want to be the "good daughter" who takes care of everything. But you are one person. If you don't set boundaries with your time, you will be pulled apart. You will become a series of fragments, scattered across everyone else's needs.

It is okay to say to an aging parent, *"I love you, and I want to help you, but I can't come over every single day."* It is okay to say to an adult child, *"I can't help you with that financial problem right now, but I can sit with you and help you make a plan."* It's not because you don't care. It's because you are one person, and you have a finite amount of light to give. If you spread it too thin, the flame goes out, and then no one has light. Your boundaries are the glass around the candle; they protect the flame from being blown out by the winds of everyone else's expectations. They ensure that you have enough energy to be the person you want to be for the people you love.

The Gentle Return to Self

As you begin to use this language, it won't feel perfect. You'll stumble. You'll say "yes" when you meant "no," and you'll find yourself over-explaining your reasons, listing three excuses when one "I can't make it" would have been enough. You'll feel the urge to send a "sorry" text five minutes after setting a limit.

That's okay. This isn't about being a master of communication or having a perfect response for every situation. It's about being more authentic in your life. It's about the slow, steady process of coming back to yourself.

We've spent so long listening to the "shoulds" of the world that our own voice has become a whisper. We've become experts at hearing what everyone else wants, but we’ve forgotten how to hear what *we* want. We've spent years living in response to other people's lives. Learning the language of boundaries is how we turn that whisper back into a conversation. It is how we remind ourselves that we are participants in our own lives, not just spectators or service providers.

The goal isn't to build walls that keep everyone out. Walls are lonely, and they eventually crumble under the pressure of isolation. The goal is to build the right kind of gates - ones that you have the key to. You decide who comes in, and you decide when it's time to close the latch and rest. You decide the terms of your own hospitality.

You’re not being "difficult." You’re not being "selfish." You’re being honest. And honestly, that is the most supportive thing you can be for yourself and for those you love. When you are clear about your boundaries, you allow others to be clear about theirs. You create a world that is a little more honest, a little more grounded, and a lot more peaceful.

It doesn't happen all at once. It happens one "no" at a time. It starts with the next conversation. It starts with the next time you feel that "yes" rising in your throat, and you decide to take a breath and wait for the truth instead. It starts when you realize that your life belongs to you. And that is a realization worth the wait.

Sustaining Change and Empowerment

The Journey from Overcommitment to Empowerment

It's a quiet kind of exhaustion. The kind that doesn't go away with a nap or a long weekend. You know the feeling - the invisible weight of being the one who holds it all together. You're the juggler, keeping every ball in the air, maintaining a rhythm that looks effortless to everyone else. But inside, you're counting the beats, wondering how much longer you can keep your arms from shaking.

In midlife, this weight often takes on a specific shape. We call it the "invisible load." It's the mental list of whose birthday is coming up, which prescription needs a refill, the unspoken tension in a friendship that needs tending, and the constant tally of what needs to be bought for dinner. It's the browser with forty tabs open, all of them titled "To Do." It often shows up in the body before we even have the words to name it. It's the tight, habitual set of your jaw when the phone vibrates on the nightstand, or the way your shoulders instinctively climb toward your ears by 10:00 AM.

We've been taught for so long that being "capable" is our highest calling - the badge of the "good woman." We take pride in being the one people call, the one who knows where everything is, the one who can "handle it."

We think that if we stop "handling it," the world will fall apart. But we rarely talk about the slow, eroding cost of that capability. It's like living in a house where you're the only one who knows how to fix the leaks, so you never get to just sit and enjoy the view. You are always on call, even in your sleep. Over time, you stop being a person and start being a resource. You become a series of solved problems rather than a human being with a pulse.

Every "yes" we give away is a small piece of our vital energy. Often, we don't even realize we're doing it; the word is out of our mouths before we've even checked in with our hearts. We think we're being helpful, or perhaps we're just doing what's expected because that's who we've always been - the reliable one, the fixer, the anchor. We say yes to the extra project at work because we want to prove we've still "got it" in an age-biased world. We say yes to the family obligation because we don't want to deal with the quiet fallout of a "no." We fear the silence that might follow a refusal, so we fill it with our labor instead. We use our "yes" to buy safety, to buy belonging, and to avoid the discomfort of other people's disappointment.

But somewhere along the way, it starts to wear you down. Each commitment becomes a stone in a back-pack you never chose to wear. Eventually, the pack gets so heavy that there's no room left for the things that actually matter - your own rest, your creative sparks, or simply the luxury of an empty hour where no one is asking anything of you. You might find yourself standing in the kitchen, staring at the wall, wondering where "you" went in the midst of all this "doing." You look at your calendar and see a list of people who need you, but you don't see a single hour for yourself.

Recognizing this isn’t a failure of character or a lack of stamina. It’s the first step toward something much kinder. It’s the realization that you cannot pour from an empty cup, no matter how much you’ve been told you should. It’s an admission that you are human, with limits that deserve to be respected. It’s finally admitting that "I can do this" is not the same as "I should do this."

It starts with paying attention to those small, sharp moments of resentment. That flicker of frustration when another email lands or another favor is asked. We often judge that resentment, calling ourselves "difficult," "cranky," or "ungrateful." But those feelings aren't enemies. They are signals from your inner self, whispering that something needs to shift. Resentment is often just the shadow of a boundary that hasn't been set. It’s a quiet protest from a heart that is tired of being last on the list. It’s the soul’s way of saying *not this.*

It’s okay to put the backpack down. In fact, it’s necessary for your survival. You don't have to carry it all to be worthy of love. Love that requires your exhaustion is not love; it’s a transaction.

The Anatomy of the Guilt Hangover

The first time you say "no," it feels like stepping into a cold wind. It’s daunting. You expect the world to stop, or for people to be deeply disappointed in you. You might experience what I call the "guilt hangover" - that lingering sense of unease the next morning, that nagging urge to call them back and say, "Actually, I can do it." You might replay the conversation over and over, looking for a way you could have said it better, or felt "nicer" about it. You might worry that you've permanently damaged a relationship by choosing your own peace over their convenience.

But guilt is often just the sound of old patterns trying to hold on. It's the "good girl" in you trying to regain control. It's socialized noise, not a moral compass. Usually, the world just keeps turning. The event goes on, the project gets handled, and the sun still sets. When you stop being the "fixer," you give others the chance to find their own solutions. You might even discover that people are more resilient than you gave them credit for.

Start small. Maybe it's a social invite that feels more like a chore than a connection. Maybe it's a committee that no longer lights you up, but you stayed on out of habit or a sense of "if I don't do it, who will?" Every time you hold a boundary, you're not building a wall; you're building a muscle. It takes practice. It takes time. But with every "no" that honors your truth, you're reclaiming a piece of your life. You are deciding that your time is a finite, precious resource - not an open-ended loan to everyone who asks. You are learning that your "yes" only has value if you are actually free to say "no."

You'll start to notice the shifts. They're subtle at first. A little less noise in your head when you wake up. A morning where you don't feel immediately behind the curve before your feet even touch the floor. A sense of peace that starts to settle in your chest, replacing that frantic "buzz" of over-stimulation. These aren't just external changes; they are the reflection of you finally deciding that your well-being matters as much as everyone else's. You begin to realize that an empowered woman cannot do everything; she is the one who knows what is worth doing.

Living with Curiosity: The Growth Perspective

Imagine moving through your day not as a performer being judged on her output, but as a curious explorer. When things don't go as planned - when a boundary slips or you find yourself overcommitted again because you got caught in a moment of people-pleasing - you don't have to meet it with the usual harsh criticism. We are so used to being our own harshest wardens, keeping a tally of every time we "gave in." But the "perfect" boundary is a myth. Life is messy, and our needs change from day to day and certainly from decade to decade.

We often think of boundaries as rigid lines, like a stone wall or a locked gate. But in reality, they are more like the banks of a river. They guide the flow, providing structure and direction, but they also adapt to the volume of the water. They move with the season.

In a season of grief, transition, or physical change - common markers of midlife - your river might need wider banks and more protection. You might need to withdraw, to say "no" to almost everything while you find your footing again. This is not weakness; it is seasonal wisdom. In a season of energy and new beginnings, you might let the flow move more freely, opening yourself to new people and projects. Sometimes the river is a trickle; sometimes it's a flood. Both are natural. Both belong.

The key is to avoid "all or nothing" thinking. If a bank overflows one day, you don't abandon the river; you just see where it needs more support. Embracing this flexibility is where the real growth happens. It allows us to see setbacks not as failures, but as valuable information. When a boundary fails, or when you find yourself back in that old habit of over-explaining your choices to someone who doesn't even need the explanation, ask yourself quietly: *What happened there? What was I trying to protect? Was I afraid of being disliked in that moment, or was I just too tired to hold the line?*

When we look at our lives with curiosity instead of judgment, the shame begins to dissolve. Shame thrives in the dark, but curiosity brings it into the light, where it can be examined. You might realize that you said "yes" to your neighbor's request because you were feeling lonely, and you wanted that moment of connection. That's not a failure; it's a human need. Once you see it, you can find a better way to meet that need without sacrificing your time.

This shift in perspective changes the atmosphere of your inner life. The fear of "doing it wrong" fades, replaced by gentle curiosity. You begin to understand that you are a work in progress, and that's a beautiful, honest thing to be. You learn to break things down into smaller, manageable steps. You celebrate the small wins - not because you've reached a final destination, but because you're moving in a direction that feels like home.

When we adopt this "beginner's mind," we stop punishing ourselves for our humanity. We realize that resilience isn't about never falling; it's about how gently we pick ourselves back up. There is a deep relief that comes when you stop trying to be the expert of your own life and start being its student. It's in that space of "not knowing" that we actually find our greatest strength. We learn that we don't need all the answers; we just need to be present for the questions.

The Myth of the Lone Wolf: Finding Your People

There is a profound shift that happens when you realize you aren't doing this alone. We spend so much of our lives - especially in our thirties and forties - trying to be strong in isolation. We convince ourselves that we should be able to handle the career, the home, the aging parents, and the internal shifts of midlife without asking for a hand. We view needing help as a crack in the armor, a sign that we've finally "let things slide." But there is a different kind of strength found in community - a collective grounding that reminds us we are seen.

The "Lone Wolf" syndrome is a cage we build for ourselves.

We think that doing it all alone proves our worth. But all we are really doing is ensuring our own exhaustion. We believe that asking for help makes us a burden. But in reality, when we refuse help, we deny others the opportunity to be there for us. We shut the door on intimacy. We think we're being strong, but we're actually being unavailable.

Imagine being in a room - or even just a long-distance phone call - where you don't have to explain why you're tired. Where your "no" is met with a nod of understanding rather than a list of follow-up questions. Where you can say, "I just can't today," and the response is, "I hear you. Me neither. Let's just sit for a minute." This kind of connection is the antidote to the frantic pace of overcommitment.

Building a network of women who are on this same path is transformative. It's about more than just sharing tips or strategies; it's about the relief of being understood without a preamble. It's about the permission we give each other to be imperfect. When we share our struggles, they lose their sharp edges. Shifting our burdens from our own shoulders to a shared space makes them feel lighter, even if the circumstances haven't changed.

Think about the specific relief of a "me too" moment. You admit that you feel resentful of your partner's free time, and your friend says, "Me too." Suddenly, the shame of that resentment starts to lift. You aren't "bad"; you're just experiencing a common struggle. This isn't about "accountability" in a clinical, goal-setting sense; it's about the warmth of knowing someone is walking a similar path. It's about the "me too" that echoes through a conversation and makes the walls of our isolation feel a little less thin. It reminds us that our feelings are not a problem to be solved, but a reality to be shared.

In midlife, friendships often change. It's a natural pruning. Some may fall away as your boundaries shift, and that can be painful. People who benefited from your lack of boundaries might not like the "new" you. They might find your new "no" inconvenient and tell you that you're "no fun" or "different." And you are. But this process also clears the space for new connections based on who you are becoming, not who you used to be.

Seek out the people who respect your journey. These are the people who won't try to "fix" your discomfort, but will simply hold the space while you navigate it. Your voice adds to the collective wisdom of the group. You aren't just taking support; you're offering it just by being honest about your own path. Sometimes, the most powerful thing you can do for another woman is to let her see you struggle and then see you try again. It's in the unmasking that we find each other.

The Ripple Effect: Why Your "No" Matters to Others

Think of a still pond at dawn. When you drop a small stone into the center, the ripples reach the edges, touching things you didn't even know were there - the reeds, the sleeping water birds, the mud at the bank.

Your boundaries work the same way. They start with you, but they don't stay there. When you begin to honor your needs, the people around you have to adjust. It can feel uncomfortable at first - for you and for them. Change usually triggers some resistance. People who were used to your "unlimited access" might be confused, frustrated, or even hurt. They might try to push back, testing the new limits to see if they're just a temporary phase or a "mood." They might try to use guilt to pull you back into your old role.

They might say things like, "But you always used to help with this," or "You've changed." And they're right. You have. And that change is a sign of health, even if it feels like tension in the moment. You are rewriting the contract of your relationships. While that causes friction, it also creates the possibility for real honesty.

But stay steady. Over time, your consistency creates a healthier environment for everyone involved. In your family, it might mean others learning how to step up because you've finally stepped back. It might mean your children - even adult children - seeing that a mother is a person with her own needs and boundaries, not just a service provider. You are showing them what self-respect looks like in action. You are teaching them that love doesn't mean infinite availability.

In your work, it might mean a culture where people actually respect each other's "off" hours because you were brave enough to stop answering emails after dinner. You're not just saving your own sanity; you're setting a new standard for the room. You are showing your colleagues that it is possible to be excellent at your job without sacrificing your entire life to it. You are helping to dismantle the "always-on" culture that is burning us all out.

The most beautiful part of this is that by modeling healthy boundaries, you are giving everyone else a permission slip to do the same. You become a beacon for those who are still drowning in their own obligations but don't know there's another way to live. Your courage to say "I can't do that right now" shows someone else - perhaps a younger colleague or a daughter - that they don't have to disappear into their to-do list either.

It wasn't an act of selfishness. It was a gift for everyone you love. You are teaching your loved ones how to treat you, and in doing so, you are teaching them how to treat themselves. This is how we change the culture of burnout - one quiet, firm boundary at a time. It's not just about you; it's about the women who are watching you, learning that it's okay to be whole. You are creating a legacy of self-respect that will ripple out far beyond your own life. You are rewriting the script for the generations who follow.

The Strength in Being Real

We spend so much time wearing masks - the "I'm fine" mask, the "I've got this" mask, the "I don't need anything" mask. We wear them to protect ourselves from judgment, and sometimes to protect others from our own messiness. We think that if we show the cracks, we'll fall apart, or that people will stop relying on us. But vulnerability is where the real connection lives. It's the courage to be real, even when it's uncomfortable.

Think of the energy it takes to keep those masks in place. It's exhausting. It's like trying to hold a beach ball underwater. Eventually, you get tired, and the ball pops up anyway. When you're honest about your limits, you invite others to be honest about theirs. It replaces the exhausting game of assumptions with the clarity of truth. It replaces performance with presence. It's a profound relief to finally say, "I'm struggling with this right now," or "I need some quiet time before I can talk about that."

Being vulnerable doesn't mean you're weak or that you've lost your footing. It means you're brave enough to let the truth be enough. It's about sharing your story with the people who have earned the right to hear it. It's about being as kind to yourself as you would be to a dear friend who was going through the same transition. You wouldn't tell her to "just push through it"; you'd tell her to take a breath. You would offer her a chair and a cup of tea. Can you offer that to yourself?

As you get more comfortable with your own "realness," you'll find that your boundaries become more natural. They stop feeling like a battle and become an extension of your integrity. You aren't "asserting" them like a soldier defending a line; you're just stating the reality of who you are. "I can't do that" becomes as simple a statement as "The sky is blue." It isn't an attack; it's just a fact.

The more you accept yourself - the flaws, the fatigue, the changing body, and the evolving mind - the less you feel the need to apologize for having needs. You realize that your value isn't tied to how useful you are to others. You are not a machine designed for maximum output. You are a human being, and you are worthy of respect simply because you are here. Dropping the mask isn't an act of defeat; it's an act of liberation. It's the moment you finally stop hiding and start living.

Celebrating the Quiet Wins

I want you to take a moment to acknowledge how far you've already come. We are so quick to look at the "gap" - the distance between where we are and where we think we should be. We focus on the times we slipped up or the boundaries we didn't hold. But I want you to look back at the "gain." I want you to see the ground you've covered. I want you to see the woman who stood her ground even when her voice shook.

We often wait for the "big" milestones to celebrate - the job change, the move, the grand resolution finally kept. But the real change, the kind that lasts, happens in the quiet, unremarkable moments of a Tuesday afternoon. It's the time you paused for three seconds before saying yes, and then said no instead. It's the evening you chose to sit on the porch and watch the light fade rather than folding that third load of laundry. It's the feeling of a Sunday that actually feels like a day of rest, rather than a frantic preparation for a week of battle.

These successes deserve to be honored. Not necessarily with a party or a grand gesture, but with a quiet, internal "thank you" to yourself. It's about building an internal library of moments where you chose yourself. Every time you honor a boundary, you're adding a volume to that library. On the days when you feel weak, or the old guilt comes knocking, you can go to that library and remember: *I know how to do this. I have done it before. I am capable of choosing my own peace.*

Savor the feeling of a respected boundary. Let it settle into your bones. It's a reminder that you are reclaiming your life, one small choice at a time. These moments are the fuel for the journey ahead. They prove that change is possible and that you are worth every bit of the effort.

Perhaps your celebration is just a few extra minutes in the garden, or a cup of tea enjoyed while it's still hot. It's the act of acknowledging: *I did that. I looked after myself.* It might be buying the flowers you like, or finally taking that walk you've been putting off because it seemed "unproductive." These rewards aren't about consumption or "treating yourself" in a superficial way; they're about connection. They are a way of telling your soul that you are finally listening. You are saying to yourself, "I see you." *Your needs matter. And I am here to protect them.*

Ritualizing the Reset

To sustain this change, we need more than just intent; we need rhythm. Midlife is often a time of high chaos, and without a rhythm to anchor us, we drift back into our old "fixing" habits.

Consider creating a small daily ritual that marks the boundary between your "public" and "private" selves. It might be changing your clothes the moment you get home, or taking five slow breaths before you walk through the front door. It could be the way you make your coffee or how you shut down your laptop at the end of the day. It might be a ten-minute walk after work to "walk off" the day's stress before you engage with your family.

These rituals are small signals to your nervous system. They say: *The work is done. You are safe now. You can come back to yourself.* They create a "buffer zone" that prevents the world's demands from bleeding into your personal peace.

Don't overthink this. It doesn't need to be elaborate. The more complicated the ritual, the less likely you are to do it. Keep it grounded. Keep it yours. The goal is to create a predictable space where you are no longer "available" to the world. It's about building a sanctuary out of the minutes of your day.

A Moment for Reflection

Once a week, perhaps on a quiet Sunday morning or before the house wakes up, find a few minutes to sit with yourself. This isn't a performance review; it's a check-in. Put away the "to-do" list and the "should" list. Light a candle if that helps you feel present. Let the silence be your companion for a while.

Don't look for "failures" or things you "should" have done better. Instead, look for the moments where you felt a sense of alignment - where your outside matched your inside. Look for the small cracks where the light started to get in.

- **When did I feel most like myself this week?** Think of a specific moment. Was it when you said no? Or when you finally asked for help? Or perhaps a moment of quiet you fought to keep? How did that feel in your body? Did your breath come easier? Did your heart feel a little lighter?

- **Where did I find a little bit of extra space?** Did you reclaim ten minutes of your morning? Did you step away from a toxic conversation or a social media scroll that was draining you? How did that extra space change your mood for the rest of the day? Did you notice the color of the sky or the sound of the wind?

· **What was the "guilt hangover" like this week, and how did I navigate it?** Did you notice the guilt and let it pass like a cloud, or did it drive you back into old habits? Did you try to "fix" a boundary you'd already set? There is no wrong answer here; there is only noticing. Every time you notice the guilt without acting on it, you are winning. Every time you stay in discomfort without apologizing, you are growing.

· **What is one small victory I can carry into tomorrow?** Write it down if you like, or just hold it in your mind. This isn't about checking a box or finishing a guide. It's about noticing the person you are becoming - someone who knows her value, honors her heart, and moves through the world with a little more grace and a lot more room to breathe.

It didn't happen all at once. It was never meant to. It's a slow unfolding, like a flower reaching for the sun. It takes time for the roots to take hold and for the petals to open. But it is happening. You are growing in ways you can't even see yet. And you are doing beautifully.

In the chapter ahead, we will look at how to maintain this resilience when life throws the inevitable curveball. Because the goal isn't to live a life without challenges; it's to build a life where you are strong enough and flexible enough to meet them without losing yourself. You are learning to be the anchor in your own storm. You are learning that your peace is a non-negotiable part of your existence.

When the Storm Actually Hits

Settling of the Dust

We tend to think that once we find our boundaries, the world will suddenly become a quieter place. There is a lovely, seductive idea we flirt with - that setting limits is like building a fence, and once the gate is locked and the latch is clicked into place, we can finally sit down on the porch and rest. We imagine a settling of the dust, a permanent state of "arriving" in which the people in our lives simply accept the new landscape and adjust their expectations accordingly.

It won't happen quite like that.

Life doesn't pause to admire your personal growth. It doesn't look at your progress and decide to go easy on you for a while. In fact, it often feels like life decides to test the structural integrity of your new foundations almost immediately. It's as if the universe wants to check: *Do you really mean it? Is this a new way of living, or just a temporary mood you're in because you read a book?*

There is a strange, almost predictable timing to it. We call it "The Honeymoon Phase of Boundaries" - that short window where you feel invincible because you haven't been tested yet. You've read the chapters, you've made the lists, and you feel a new kind of steel in your spine. But eventually, the weather shifts. The air grows heavy. The unglamorous reality of midlife - the messy, noisy, demanding reality - comes knocking.

Just as you start to feel steady, a family member calls with an "emergency" that, if you look closely, isn't yours to fix. It's the brother who needs money again for a problem he refuses to solve, or the sister who needs you to drop everything for a drama she created. Work demands more of you just as you've decided to give less - a last-minute project lands on your desk at 4:55 PM, precisely when you'd promised yourself you'd be home for a quiet dinner and a bath. A friend reacts with a sharp, cold edge when you use that new, slightly unfamiliar word: *no*.

And there it is. The storm.

It arrives not to punish you, but because that is simply what life does. It moves. It pushes. It tests the edges of anything that tries to stay still. In midlife, these storms often carry a specific, heavy weight - the "sandwich" pressure of aging parents who need more care than they'll admit, and adult children who haven't quite found their feet. You are the middle ground, the one everyone looks to for the "yes" that keeps their world spinning.

In those moments, everything you've been practicing in the quiet of your journal or the safety of your therapy sessions is suddenly required of you all at once. You aren't just reading about boundaries anymore; you are breathing them. And it feels much harder, much more visceral, than it did on the page.

The Old Reflex Will Knock First

When the pressure rises, your nervous system doesn't go looking for your latest insights or the clever phrasing you practiced in the mirror. It doesn't remember the "empowering" quote you saved on your phone. It reaches for what it knows. It reaches for survival.

For many of us, survival was built on being the one who makes things okay. From a very young age, you might have been the one who could read the temperature of a room before you even stepped into it. You learned to scan faces for a hint of irritation, to watch the set of a jaw or the squint of an eye. You learned to absorb the tension, to be the lubricant in the gears of a complicated family or a demanding office. You learned that saying "yes" before the request was even finished was the fastest way to feel safe, valued, or at least ignored.

This is the "fawn" response - a physiological softening meant to disarm conflict before it even starts. It's the way your voice goes up half an octave when someone is angry. It's the way you smile even when you're hurt. It's the headache that starts behind your eyes the moment you agree to something you hate.

The old reflex is a quiet, persistent thing. It whispers. *Just say yes this once. It's easier if I don't make a fuss. I can deal with the fallout later - I'm good at carrying things.*

If we're being honest, there is a certain comfort in that reflex. It's familiar. Predictable. It's been your companion for decades. Choosing it feels like slipping on an old wool jumper - the one that doesn't quite fit anymore and makes your skin itch, but it's there, hanging in the cupboard, and you know exactly how it feels. You know how to play the "good girl." You know how to be the "reliable one." There is a strange, addictive safety in being the one everyone can count on, even if it's killing you. You might even feel a brief, warm rush of approval when you agree to help, a momentary high of being "needed," even as your own heart begins to sink into your shoes.

But you know, too, that it still shrinks you.

It wasn't weakness that built that reflex. It was a younger version of you doing your best to navigate a world that demanded your compliance. You were brave in your own way, using "yes" as a shield to protect your peace. But that jumper doesn't fit the woman you are becoming. It's tight across the chest. It's restrictive. And while the reflex promises safety, it no longer offers peace. You are beginning to realize that "peace" bought with self-betrayal is just a different kind of war - one that you fight silently against yourself every single day.

Resilience Isn't About Getting It Right

I see so many women quietly give up here. They hit the storm, they wobble, and they decide they've failed. They think resilience is a performance - a state of being where you are always calm, always firm, and always holding your ground with perfect poise. They imagine themselves standing like a statue against the wind, unmoving and untouched, speaking their boundaries in a voice that never shakes and eyes that never blink.

It isn't that. It can't be that, because we are human.

Resilience is not perfection. It is the act of returning.

Think about a meditation practice. You don't "succeed" when your mind stays perfectly still for twenty minutes. That's not the point. You succeed every time you notice your mind has wandered to the grocery list or a conversation from three years ago, and you gently, without judgment, bring it back to your breath. Boundary work is exactly the same. The "work" is the return.

It's that moment, perhaps mid-sentence, where you realize you've just agreed to a commitment that makes your stomach tight. You can feel the resentment already starting to bloom, a bitter taste in the back of your throat. In the past, you would have followed through out of shame, even if it meant staying up until midnight or canceling your own doctor's appointment. You would have cursed yourself the whole time, but you would have done it.

Now, resilience looks like pausing. It's catching yourself in the middle of the slip. It's having the courage to stop the momentum and say, "Actually, I spoke too soon. I felt a pressure to say yes, but I need to look at my calendar and get back to you."

The "return" doesn't even have to happen in the moment. Sometimes resilience is sending a text three hours later - or even three days later - that says, "I realized after we spoke that I don't actually have the capacity to help with the bake sale this weekend. I'm sorry for the confusion."

That is not a failure; that is a victory. It is the act of valuing your truth over your image. Every time you return, you make the path back to yourself a little more well-worn. You are telling your brain: *We don't live in the old jumper anymore.* You are teaching yourself that you are allowed to change your mind.

The Pause Is Your Power

When things speed up, your body will want to match that pace. It's an evolutionary response - fight, flight, or fix. You'll feel the urge to soothe the other person's disappointment before it turns into anger. You'll want to solve the problem before it creates a ripple that touches you. We've been conditioned to think that speed equals competence and that an immediate response is the ultimate sign of care.

But speed is often the enemy of intention. When we move too fast, we move from habit, not from choice. We are on autopilot, and autopilot only knows the old routes.

This is where the work actually happens, not in the grand declarations of "never again," but in the tiny, almost invisible spaces. It's the three seconds between a question and an answer. It's the space where you decide if you are responding or reacting. This pause is where you check your "internal weather." Does this request feel like an expansion in your chest, or does it feel like a heavy, cold weight in your solar plexus?

Think about the phone ringing. You see the name. You know they want something - a favor, a listening ear for the same problem they've had for ten years, a "quick" task that isn't quick. The old you would have picked up immediately, already preparing the "yes" before the greeting was over.

The new practice is simpler: you let it ring. You take a breath. You look at the phone and you ask yourself, *Do I have the capacity for this right now?* Not, *do I have the "time,"* but *do I have the "room"?* Maybe you're sitting at your kitchen table with a cup of tea. Maybe the sun is hitting the floor in a way you want to enjoy for just five more minutes. That is enough of a reason. A moment of silence after a request is made, instead of the immediate "Of course." A simple, "I need a little time to think about that." A deep breath before you hit "send" on an email that feels like an over-commitment.

The pause interrupts the script. It breaks the old loop. It gives you just enough room to see that you have a choice. And choice is where your power quietly sits, waiting for you to notice it. Without the pause, you are just a collection of reactions. With it, you are a person. You are giving yourself the dignity of a second thought, and in doing so, you are teaching others that your time is a resource, not a communal well.

Not Everyone Will Like the New You

We should talk about this part gently, but we have to be honest. This is often the hardest part of the reset. It's the part people don't always tell you about in the motivational quotes.

When you stop over-giving, people will notice. And not all of them will celebrate it. This isn't necessarily because they are "toxic" or "bad" people; it's because the dynamic of the relationship has shifted. You are no longer playing the role that made their lives easier, and that change can feel like a loss to them. You were the "reliable one," the "fixer," the "constant," and now you are becoming "unpredictable."

To someone who is used to your compliance, your boundary feels like an attack. To these people, your "no" feels like a withdrawal of love. They might start "Testing the Fence." They might try different tactics - anger, guilt, or even a sudden, overwhelming "need" - to see if they can get the old you back.

People who have grown used to your constant availability might feel confused. They might get irritated. They might even try to pull you back into the old "yes" through subtle pressure. They might say things like, "You've changed," or "You used to be so much easier to talk to," or "I don't know who you are anymore." They might use the silent treatment, or a sharp tone, or a heavy sigh to try and "correct" your behavior back to what is comfortable for them.

And they're right. You *have* changed. You are becoming someone who respects herself as much as she respects others. You are moving from a "contract" of compliance to a "covenant" of honesty.

It's important to remember: this doesn't mean your boundary is wrong. It means it's working. It means you have finally stopped carrying the weight that belonged to someone else, and that they are finally feeling the weight of their own lives. That discomfort is theirs to manage, not yours to fix. If you fix it for them, you rob them of their own growth.

It's unsettling for them, yes. But it's also unsettling for you. There is a certain grief in realizing that some people only liked the version of you that didn't have needs. It's hard to be the one who changes the dance. You might feel lonely for a while. You might feel like the "bad guy" in a story you didn't write. Just remember that you aren't responsible for their comfort at the expense of your own soul. If your relationship depended on your silence, it wasn't much of a relationship to begin with. It was just a performance.

You Can Be Kind Without Being Available

There is a quiet shift that happens when you realize these two things aren't the same. For years, we've been taught that kindness is synonymous with compliance. We think that being "good" means being "available." We've been told that a "good woman" is one whose door is always open and whose cup is always being poured out. We confuse "nice" (which is often just a mask we wear to be liked) with "kind" (which is an honest movement of the heart).

But you can care deeply for someone and still say no to their request. You can be a loving person and still have a closed door.

Think of a lighthouse. Its purpose is to shine a light, to provide direction, to keep others from crashing into the rocks. But the lighthouse doesn't run out into the water to save the boats. It doesn't throw itself into the surf. It stays on its foundation. It remains anchored on the shore. If the lighthouse tried to be everywhere at once, or if it ran toward every boat, its light would go out. It would be destroyed by the very thing it's trying to help. Its power lies in its stillness.

Kindness isn't measured by how much of yourself you set on fire to keep others warm. It's measured by how honestly you show up. When you say, "I wish I could help, but I can't take that on right now," you are being kind to them by being honest, and to yourself by being real. You are refusing to build a relationship on a lie.

You are saying, "I want to help you from a place of abundance, not from a place of debt."

You say yes. Even when something in you says no. And somewhere along the way, it starts to wear you down. You become brittle. You become resentful. That resentment eventually leaks out anyway - in sharp comments, in avoiding people, in the way you sigh when the phone rings. Eventually, you become unavailable anyway because you've burnt out.

Honesty is a deeper form of love than compliance ever was. It's a love that allows both people to stand on their own two feet. It says, "I love you enough to be real with you, even if it's uncomfortable."

When You Do Slip (Because You Will)

There will be days when exhaustion wins. There will be moments when the social pressure is too high, or your child is crying, or your boss is looming, and you'll slip. You'll say yes out of habit, or guilt, or simply because you didn't have the energy to explain yourself. You'll find yourself at a volunteer event you hate, or hosting a dinner you're too tired to cook, wondering how you got there.

This is not a reason to turn on yourself. It is not evidence that you haven't "learned anything" or that you're back at square one. It is just information. It is data.

Instead of a post-mortem of your failures, try a little curiosity. *Were you tired? Were you caught off guard? Was it a person who has always been a "blind spot" for you - someone whose approval you still find yourself craving?*

Maybe you realize you can't make decisions after 8:00 PM because your resolve is too low. Maybe you realize you need to text a certain person because their voice triggers your "fixer" reflex. Every slip is a map. It shows you where the terrain is still a bit rocky.

Next time, you'll recognize the feeling in your chest - that specific tightening of the throat, that hollow feeling in your solar plexus - a few seconds sooner. And those seconds are where your freedom lives. Resilience grows here - not in getting it perfect, but in understanding your patterns with a little more compassion each time. It doesn't happen all at once. It happens in the return.

The Anchor in the Tide

We talked before about becoming the anchor in your own storm. But we need to be clear about what an anchor actually does. An anchor doesn't stop the ocean from moving. It doesn't calm the waves or make the wind stop blowing. The tide will still pull. The world will still be demanding. Your family will still have needs. The aging parent will still be aging.

The anchor is just there to make sure you aren't swept away.

You are allowed to feel overwhelmed. You are allowed to feel wobbly and unsure. Strength, in this season of your life, isn't about being rigid. It isn't about being a rock that nothing can touch. Rocks break under enough pressure. They crack. They erode. They are worn down by the constant friction of the world until they are just sand.

True strength is more like the willow. It has roots that go deep, deep into the earth - that's your internal sense of self, your values, your quiet "no." Those roots are the promises you've made to yourself. But its branches are flexible. They can sway in the wind. They can bend when the storm hits. They don't fight the air; they move with it, always returning to the center once the gust has passed.

You are allowed to be messy. You are allowed to say, "This is hard for me." You are allowed to be a work in progress. Strength is the ability to be flexible without losing your foundation. It's about having roots that go deep enough to let you sway without breaking. It's the "strength of the return." It's the ability to say, "I am bent, but I am not broken."

A Quiet Promise

So when the next storm arrives - and we both know it will - you don't need to handle it perfectly. You don't need to be the calmest person in the room. You don't need to have the perfect "boundary script" ready to go.

You only need to remember this: Pause. Check in. Choose.

Even if your voice shakes. Even if you have to call back five minutes later to change your answer. Even if you have to go into the bathroom and cry for a minute before you come back out and say "no" again.

Every time you choose yourself honestly, you are reinforcing something much deeper than a boundary. You are reinforcing trust. You are showing that little girl inside you - the one who learned to survive by disappearing, by being small, by being "easy," by carrying everyone else's heavy emotions - that she is safe now. That you are looking out for her. That you won't trade her peace for someone else's comfort.

You are telling her that her life is finally her own. You are making a promise to stay with yourself, even when the wind picks up. You are finally, after all these years, becoming your own best friend. You are reparenting the part of you that thought she had to be a martyr to be loved.

You are building trust in yourself. And that trust is the only thing that can truly hold you steady.

Before You Turn the Page...

Take a second to see how far you've already come. You are reading this because you're tired of the old ways. You are no longer saying yes without feeling that nudge in your spirit. You are no longer abandoning yourself without at least noticing the cost. You are noticing the itch of the old jumper. You are noticing the way your body reacts when you over-commit. You are waking up.

It wasn't weakness. It was survival. But you are moving beyond survival now. You are moving into presence. You are moving into a life that is actually yours, shaped by your choices rather than your reactions.

That alone is a quiet kind of strength. It doesn't need to be loud to be real. It doesn't need an audience to be valid. It is a private revolution, fought in the three-second spaces of your day. It's the silent victory of a deep breath.

Conclusion

We've reached the last few pages of this time together.

I'd like us to just sit for a moment before you close the cover. We've walked through a lot of heavy terrain - the kind that usually stays hidden under the surface of our busy lives, tucked away under "to-do" lists and the needs of everyone else. Learning to set boundaries isn't a quick fix or a neat trick you pick up in a weekend. It's an art. It's a slow, intentional unlearning of everything we were told a "good woman" should be. And for most of us, it's a language we were never taught to speak.

I wrote this because I've seen what happens when we don't have those lines in place. I've seen the way the eyes go dull from exhaustion and the way resentment starts to poison even the relationships we love most. I've lived it, too. I know the feeling of waking up at 3:00 a.m. with a racing heart, wondering how I'm going to fulfill a promise I never should have made.

This isn't a set of rules to follow or a checklist to tick off. It's a way to find your breath again. We've talked about the weight of guilt - that heavy, damp blanket that settles over us the moment we consider putting ourselves first. We've looked at that familiar, sharp edge of fear that comes when we think about saying no. It's a physical thing, isn't it? That tightness in the throat, that instinct to apologize before we've even done anything wrong.

If there is one thing I hope you carry with you, it's this: saying no isn't about being difficult. It's about being honest. When we say "yes" while our insides are screaming "no," we aren't being kind. We're being dishonest. Setting a boundary is a way of telling yourself, and the world, that your peace matters just as much as anyone else's. It's acknowledging that you are a person, not a resource.

Over these chapters, we looked at the "yes" that leaves you empty. We unpicked the knots of people-pleasing and tried to understand where those habits started - the stories from our families, the cultural whispers that told us our value was tied to our usefulness, and the quiet expectations we've carried for decades. We realized that many of these patterns weren't choices we made consciously; they were scripts handed to us before we were old enough to know better.

It wasn't weakness that brought you here. It was survival. You learned to be small, or quiet, or endlessly accommodating because that was how you kept things moving. That was how you stayed safe. But maybe, finally, you're realizing that you don't have to just survive anymore. There is a different way to live - one where you don't have to set yourself on fire just to keep everyone else warm.

We've practiced the words. We've looked at the ways we can speak up without feeling like we're starting a war. We explored how it feels to lead with empathy - both for the person standing in front of you and, more importantly, for the woman in the mirror. Empathy doesn't mean you have to say yes to every request. It means you understand why they're asking, but you also understand why you can't give it.

A boundary isn't a wall meant to shut the world out. It's a door with a lock, and you hold the key. It's what allows you to let the right things in - connection, respect, genuine joy - and keep the things that drain you out. When you have clear limits, you aren't pushing people away. You're actually inviting them into a real relationship. You're showing them who you actually are, not the hollowed-out version of yourself you've been presenting. It's a gift to them, too, though they might not see it that way at first.

I want to encourage you to take this slowly. Don't feel like you have to change every relationship overnight. That's how burnout happens.

Try it tomorrow. Just once. Maybe with a small thing - a coffee invitation you don't want to accept, or a task at work that isn't yours to carry. You might feel that rush of heat in your chest - the discomfort of change. Your mind might start spinning with justifications and apologies. Let it be there. Don't try to push the discomfort away. It's just a sign that you're doing something new. It's the feeling of a muscle being used for the first time.

Every time you say no to something that wears you down, you're saying yes to the version of you that is finally allowed to rest. You're saying yes to an extra hour of sleep, or a quiet walk, or simply the mental space to think your own thoughts. That isn't selfish. It's preservation. You cannot pour from an empty cup, and you certainly cannot be the presence you want to be in the world if you are constantly running on fumes.

This isn't the end of the work. It's just the beginning of a different way of moving through the world. It's a lifelong process of noticing when you've given too much and learning how to pull back. It doesn't happen all at once. There will be days when you slip back into old habits, and that's okay. Be gentle with yourself on those days. The goal isn't perfection; it's awareness.

I'm so grateful you let me sit beside you for this part of your journey. I wrote this for the women who are tired of being the anchor while everyone else sails. I wrote it for the ones who feel invisible in their own lives. Your willingness to look at these pages and see yourself in them - to admit that things need to change - that takes a quiet, steady kind of courage. It's easier to stay numb. It's harder to wake up and decide you're worth the effort.

As you move into whatever comes next, keep the tools we've talked about close by. Put them in your pocket. You aren't alone in this. There is a whole community of us, all learning how to use our voices again, all figuring out where we end, and others begin. We are all unlearning the same silence.

Thank you for trusting me with your time and your heart. I hope these words have felt like a bit of a lifeline, or at least a permission slip to be a little kinder to yourself. You've spent so long being kind to everyone else. It's time you turned some of that warmth inward.

Take care of the seeds you've planted here. They might seem small now, but they have a way of taking root. Let them grow into a life where you are heard, where your needs have a seat at the table, and where you finally have the space to just be you. Not the "you" they expect, but the "you" that has been waiting under the surface all this time.

Here's to the quiet, steady freedom that's waiting for you. It's closer than you think.

My GIFT To You

And if you'd like a little laughter to travel with the lessons in these pages, I've created a bonus set of printable cards just for you. These cheeky, light-hearted cards are filled with warm humor and boundary-loving wit...perfect for pinning on the fridge, slipping into a friend's handbag, popping into a greeting card, or keeping nearby as a gentle reminder that saying no can come with a smile. Sometimes the strongest messages are the ones that make us laugh first.

Just scan the code below for access:

Make a Difference with Your Review

Ulock the Power of Generosity

"Every time we honor the truth of our own experience, we quietly give someone else permission to honor theirs."
— Natalie Mills

A Little Note Before You Close the Cover... Your Turn to Choose What Stays – and What Goes

Have you ever found yourself in a moment where something inside you shifted – quietly, but unmistakably?
A point where the old way of saying yes no longer felt right... yet saying no still felt unfamiliar?

That space – right there – is where this book lives.

The Art of Saying No was written for that exact moment. Not to turn you into someone harder, sharper, or less caring – but to help you return to yourself.

To pause before the automatic yes.
To listen for what is actually true.
To choose your next step with honesty... and just enough courage to follow it through.

And perhaps, along the way, to realise this:
Saying no isn't the end of connection.

It's the beginning of a more honest one – including the one you have with yourself.

Now you can help the next reader who's standing right where you once stood – curious, maybe a little restless, and ready for a gentle nudge.

Why your review matters

By sharing a few honest sentences, you can help another woman:

Realize she's not alone in the messy, beautiful middle years

Discover simple tools for calm, clarity, and self-kindness

Feel brave enough to rewrite her own story – one mindful step at a time

It only takes a minute

Pop over to the review section where you found this book and jot a few genuine words:

What resonated most for you?

Which practice or story lit a spark?

Why would you recommend this book to someone navigating midlife?

OR use this link:
https://www.amazon.com/review/review-your-purchases/?asin=1923524275

Hit **Submit** and know you've just left a trail of encouragement – like a warm cup of tea waiting for the next traveler.

Thank you, from the bottom of my midlife-mischief-loving heart, for helping other women discover their own fresh start.

With gratitude,
Natalie Mills
Author of *The Art Of Saying No*

www.ingramcontent.com/pod-product-compliance
Lightning Source LLC
LaVergne TN
LVHW020046110826
845155LV00029B/654

* 9 7 8 1 9 2 3 5 2 4 2 7 9 *